# Chère Annette

## Letters from Russia

## 1820–1828

Anna Pavlovna

# Chère Annette

## Letters from Russia

## 1820–1828

*The Correspondence of the Empress
Maria Feodorovna of Russia
to her daughter
the Grand Duchess Anna Pavlovna,
the Princess of Orange*

Edited by

S.W. JACKMAN

ALAN SUTTON

Dutch edition first published in Holland in 1990 by Bosch & Keuning nv, Baarn

First published in the United Kingdom in 1994
Alan Sutton Publishing Limited
Phoenix Mill · Far Thrupp · Stroud · Gloucestershire

First published in the United States of America in 1994
Alan Sutton Publishing Inc
83 Washington Street · Dover · NH 03820

British Library Cataloguing in Publication Data

A catalogue record for this book is available from the British Library.

ISBN 0–7509–0552–2

Library of Congress Cataloging in Publication Data applied for

Typeset in 10/14 Baskerville.
Typesetting and origination by
Alan Sutton Publishing Limited.
Printed and bound in Great Britain by
The Bath Press, Bath, Avon.

# Contents

# List of Plates

*Frontispiece*: Anna Pavlovna, a portrait miniature by A. Delatour, 1819

*Between pp. 84 and 85:*

The author and publisher would like to thank the following for their kind permission to reproduce illustrations: Hulton Deutsch Collection (No. 6); Royal House Archives Trust, The Hague (*Frontispiece* and Nos 2, 3, 4, 5, 7, 8); SCR Library (No. 1).

# *Acknowledgements*

I wish to express my thanks and appreciation to Her Majesty The Queen of The Netherlands for permission to publish the correspondence of the Empress Maria Feodorovna of Russia to her daughter Anna Pavlovna, the Princess of Orange. These letters are part of Her Majesty's collection in the Korinklifk Hieusarchief in The Hague. I am also most appreciative of Her Majesty's kindness in allowing me to reproduce illustrative material from royal portraits in her possession.

I am also indebted to the following individuals for assistance: Madame Bérangère Steel, Madam Angéle Segger, Professor G.V. Downes, Dr B. Woelderink, Dr Coenraad Tamse, Cornelis and Marianne Willems, Robbert Ammerlaan, Arjen Lobach and Geoffrey Skelsey. Roger Thorp and Jane Singleton, my editors, have been most helpful. To all of the above I wish to express my appreciation. Finally I should like to thank the master, fellows and staff of St Edmund's College, Cambridge for their kind and generous hospitality.

S.W.J.
Cambridge, England
Victoria, Canada

# Introduction

Personal documents, such as letters and diaries, are valuable sources for social history because of their liveliness and readability. Private correspondence has a peculiar attraction because, unlike a journal or diary, there is an acknowledged recipient to read and react to the letter itself in a very direct and immediate fashion. Particularly fascinating are those letters between intimates, be they familial or amatory. The ability to write a good letter was a sign of being an educated person, and it was an act of artistic creation. The purpose of correspondence was not merely to inform one person of the life of another, nor was it just to provide a means of retaining contact, but the letter was thought to be the most appropriate vehicle to express ideas and sentiments. With the tyranny of distance imposing itself, the letter was an alternative to direct social intercourse and private conversation.

Leisured individuals spent many hours each day at the desk writing to friends and relations. Royal personages, surrounded as they were by legions of domestic servants and free from the mundane activities of daily life, had even more time to devote to their correspondence. Moreover, while they, like lesser mortals, discussed personal matters, they were also able to comment in a knowledgeable fashion on the wider scene – social and political – from a special vantage point and in a manner that was not possible to the ordinary citizen.

The letters of the Empress Maria Feodorovna to her daughter, Anna Pavlovna, the Princess of Orange, provide a very special insight into life encompassing the Romanov dynasty both in Russia and in The Netherlands. The last years of Alexander I and the early years of Nicholas I are discussed in this correspondence. However, the letters are not exclusively political; they also express the sentiments and the concerns of a mother for the welfare of a favourite daughter and her family far away from her place of birth.

Maria Feodorovna was the name taken by Sophia Dorothea of Wurttemberg when she became a member of the Russian imperial family and joined the Russian Orthodox Church. She was the daughter of Duke Frederick of Wurttemberg and a niece of King Frederick the Great of Prussia.

She was born in 1759 at Stettin where her father was in command of the garrison. Interestingly enough, her future mother-in-law, Catherine the Great, had also been born in Stettin, had been called Sophia and was a protégé of the Prussian monarch. Sophia Dorothea was a well-educated and attractive young woman when she was selected by the Russian sovereign to be the wife of her heir, the Grand Duke Paul. He had been married previously, but his first wife had died in childbirth.

The Wurttemberg princess was a member of the junior branch of the grand ducal family and, consequently, without the duties of a reigning house. Her father Frederick maintained a cultivated and sophisticated court at his residence at Étupes and Montbéliard. Sophia Dorothea was encouraged in her artistic and intellectual tastes by her family circle and she was to bring these attributes to her husband's country. She was to cultivate the arts, to become the patroness of a number of educational bodies in Russia and to establish at Pavlovsk an entourage that reflected her interests. The youthful princess was not beautiful, but she had charm and a desire to please. Finding herself in a great imperial court, she was very conscious of rank and position, and she always felt constrained to put her duties as a princess to the fore at the expense of private sentiment.

Paul Petrovitch, her husband, was a very different sort of individual. He was a curious *mélange* and views of him are totally contradictory. There were those who saw him as 'the true son of the enlightenment', and one who might have made Russia into a modern state by playing the role of 'the enlightened despot'. Others believed him to be the victim of a twisted inheritance, namely the mental instability of the earlier Romanovs and the Dukes of Holstein. He was aged twenty-two when he met his bride in Berlin and initially the young couple were happy and contented. Two sons were born soon after the marriage, the elder, Alexander, in 1777 and the second, Constantine, in 1778. The two boys were removed from their parents' control by their imperious grandmother, the Empress Catherine, and were to be educated according to her ideas of the role and duties of princes.

In 1781 the grand ducal couple made a trip to Vienna, Paris, Venice and various German states. The Empress Catherine bade them farewell, saying, 'Go and travel and then come back to Russia – when you see your own country again you will be filled with new ideas. . . . I trust you may reap such good from your travels that you will both be ennobled thereby to be of greater service to others.' The travellers made an agreeable impression wherever they went. They were officially incognito, using the titles of the Count and Countess du Nord, but everyone knew who they were and they were received with all the deference due to their rank. Among the places they visited was the village of Zandaam, where they inspected the house inhabited by Peter the Great during his sojourn in The Netherlands to learn the art of shipbuilding.

Paul and Maria Feodorovna were away from St Petersburg for about fourteen months. Upon their return, they resumed their life as it had been prior to their departure. Maria Feodorovna particularly liked their residence of Pavlovsk, which she was determined to create a sort of Russian Trianon. It was at Pavlovsk that she was to spend her happiest hours, as her letters to her daughter later indicate; she embellished the palace in a handsome manner with elegant furniture and splendid pictures. (Curiously, an historian, K. Waliszewski, writing in Russia early in the twentieth century, declared that Maria Feodorovna's taste was 'mediocre', a view which would not be accepted today.) The Grand Duke Paul favoured Gatchina – a sort of Russian Potsdam – which was a massive residence without much charm. He amused himself drilling his soldiers – like his father Emperor Peter III, he was a slavish admirer of Frederick the Great – and his wife, when present, planned theatricals and picnics to amuse her husband and his entourage.

Over the next decade the imperial couple were to have five daughters: Alexandra (1783), Helena (1784), Maria (1786), Catherine (1788) and Anna (1795). Their grandmother had mixed feelings about this 'regiment of females', but she was sufficiently interested in their welfare to appoint as *gouvernante* Charlotte Lieven, 'the dear and good countess', who was to become an intimate friend of the entire family. The family circle was to be enlarged further by the birth of two sons, Nicholas (1796) and Michael (1798); their advent pleased the Empress Catherine rather more. There were vast differences in age between the two elder sons and the rest of the family. Anna Pavlovna was seventeen years younger than her eldest brother. She and her two siblings, Nicholas and Michael, were particularly close and as children they formed a secret society called *The Triopathy* (their mother was to be an honorary member) and they had special rings which they wore for the rest of their lives to remind them of this bond.

In 1796 the Empress Catherine died and the Grand Duke Paul succeeded to the throne. One of his first acts was to issue a decree declaring that no longer would the sovereign be able to nominate his successor – at one time it had been mooted that the late ruler had contemplated naming her grandson Alexander as her heir rather than her son. This act of the new monarch was to have serious consequences some three decades later. In addition he stated that no woman could assume the Russian throne.

Sadly, the married life of the Emperor and his wife had become less happy. He consoled himself with various mistresses. He neglected his family and began to see them as enemies. He became increasingly paranoic and in the spring of 1801 it would seem that he seriously considered confining his wife in a convent and imprisoning his two elder sons, Alexander in the same prison at Ropsha where Ivan VI had been murdered, and Constantine in the Fortress of St Peter and St Paul. The Emperor's behaviour became so erratic and irresponsible that a group of nobles – many of them formerly high in the councils of the Empress Catherine – with the concurrence of the Grand Duke Alexander proposed to place the sovereign under arrest, force his abdication and restore political rationality to Russia. The plotters invaded the royal apartments in the Michael Palace on the night of 11 March 1801, a scuffle ensued, and in the process Paul was strangled. His eldest son, upon receiving the news of his father's demise, was exceedingly distressed but after some argument he accepted the Crown. For a brief time, when Maria Feodorovna heard that her husband had been murdered, it would appear that she assumed the imperial power would devolve upon herself. Finally, she accepted the situation and formally acknowledged her son's accession to the throne, but for the rest of his life Alexander gave his mother much deference and considerable authority. It was from this time the Emperor's mother had precedence over his wife – a state of affairs that continued until 1917.

Once Alexander had been crowned and the outward demonstrations of mourning and regret for the deceased sovereign had been followed, Maria Feodorovna settled into an agreeable pattern of life, moving from Pavlovsk to Gatchina to Czarskoeselo to the Winter Palace. Each year she went through the motions of saying prayers for the repose of the soul of her late husband, and she reminded her offspring to do likewise, but it would seem that she had acquired the serenity that was to be an essential aspect of her character. However, she retained the blood-stained night-shirt of her murdered husband. This she kept in a crystal reliquary in her private apartments. Whenever she travelled she always took the hat that had belonged to Emperor Paul. She supervised the education of her younger children and she played a not-unimportant role in international politics by refusing to give her consent to

Napoleon's proposal of marriage to either of her daughters, Catherine or Anna. The reason given for this rejection was somewhat specious, namely that their older sisters, Alexandra and Helena, having married overly young, had died in childbirth. This attitude taken by Maria Feodorovna was entirely in accord with the feelings of her son, the Emperor.

Maria Feodorovna, like most of her contemporaries, was constantly concerned to find suitable consorts for her daughters. It was necessary that they be *ebengebürtig*, that is, of equal rank. The eldest daughter, Alexandra, had married Archduke Joseph, Helena had espoused the Grand Duke Frederick of Mecklenbourg Schwerin, Maria was the wife of the Grand Duke Charles of Saxe-Weimar, while Catherine (to escape from Napoleon) had become the wife of George the Grand Duke of Oldenburg, and upon his demise, she married King William of Wurttemberg. Only Anna Pavlovna remained unwed and her happiness was a matter of concern for her mother. One potential suitor was the Duke de Berri, the heir presumptive of King Louis XVIII of France, but there were difficulties as he was a Roman Catholic. Luckily, a more attractive potential spouse was discovered.

In 1814, when the Emperor Alexander was in England, he met the Prince of Orange. The latter was at one time a prospective husband for Princess Charlotte, the heiress to the British throne, but this had come to nothing. The Prince of Orange was charming, handsome and well mannered; he had an excellent reputation and was a good soldier (he was to fight gallantly at Waterloo) and he was the heir to the newly established Kingdom of The Netherlands. Moreover, he was a Protestant and the religious barriers were not insuperable; he and his family had no objection to a wife whose adherence to the Russian Orthodox Church was to continue. Moreover, the possibility of an alliance between the Russian imperial family and the Dutch royal house was exceedingly flattering to the latter. Late in 1815 a formal marriage contract was drawn up: the bride was to receive a million roubles from the Emperor as a dowry – her prospective father-in-law, King William I, agreed to pay 5 per cent interest on the money to give her an adequate income – and she was also to receive very large sums annually from the so-called appanage fund established by her father. Over the years letters from St Petersburg allude to money paid from what was called, 'The Lombards'. Indeed, Anna Pavlovna was a very wealthy young woman.

The Prince of Orange went to St Petersburg in 1816 for the nuptial ceremony which took place on 21 February. The youthful bridegroom became a very favourite member of his wife's family. The newly married pair remained in Russia for some months, only returning to The Netherlands in early summer. They were given a palace in Brussels and a residence in The Hague.

King William I of The Netherlands and his consort, Queen Wilhelmina, made the bride very welcome, as did her young sister-in-law, Marianne, and her brother-in-law, Frederick. Life at the Dutch court was far more simple than the grandeur and elegance of St Petersburg. Indeed, Anna Pavlovna was to prefer the establishment in Brussels where she could play a more glamorous role.

Although separated from her Russian relations by vast distances, Anna Pavlovna kept in close touch with her mother and brothers with a steady stream of letters. In return, she received from their responses news of their activities. Her most assiduous correspondent, naturally enough, was her mother, who wrote to her favourite daughter every day. Some of the letters were very brief, having almost a journal-like quality. Others were lengthy but always visible was the affection of *Maman* for her *Chère Annette*. Consequently, Anna Pavlovna was very *au courant* with life in Russia.

In 1819, much to the delight of the Empress Maria Feodorovna, she was able to see her beloved daughters Maria and Anna again. She was to make extended visits to Weimar and The Netherlands. This renewal of family ties brought pleasure to all. Moreover, the Empress was able to observe for herself the world in which her youngest daughter lived and to understand her situation in a country with more liberal traditions than was the situation in Russia. Upon her return to St Petersburg, the flow of correspondence began anew; mother and daughter wrote regularly as before. The letters written from the summer of 1816 to 1819 do not seem to have survived. They may well have been lost in the fire which destroyed the residence in Brussels of the Prince and Princess of Orange in 1820. It would seem from the comments of Maria Feodorovna to her daughter that the latter was not always overly careful with her possessions (the loss of some of the jewellery in the conflagration through apparent carelessness is a case in point) but it may well be that the earlier letters were in fact deposited in the princess's library, which was totally destroyed, while the more recent correspondence was in her private apartments and rescued. At any rate, those letters which have not been lost, that is, from 1820 to 1828, are fascinating.

Every year in January, Maria Feodorovna began with sending greetings to her daughter for her name day. In addition to personal felicitations, presents accompanied her letter. The gifts were often handsome pieces of jewellery or money. At the same time, payments for the princess's income from the appanage fund were paid. Indeed, Anna Pavlovna's money from the latter was in excess of one hundred thousand guilders per annum. In addition, Anna Pavlovna was reminded in mid-March each year to pray for the repose of her father's soul. Her mother regarded this dolorous time as being worthy of note, and requiring special attention. Otherwise there is no particular pattern to the style and content of the letters.

The activities of the Emperor Alexander were recounted reasonably frequently. Sometimes he was referred to by name and sometimes by his title. Maria Feodorovna, like all members of the imperial family, gave great deference to the reigning monarch. The Empress Elizabeth, Alexander's wife, is referred to only incidentally, always by her title and never by her personal name. Indeed, she and her mother-in-law were not overly sympathetic and it was thought by contemporaries that the latter may well have preferred Maria Naryshkin, her son's mistress, to his wife. However, good manners forbear her to say any such thing in writing. Much was said about Nicholas (often referred to as Nix or Nikki) and his wife, Alexandra (periodically called by the diminutive Sachine). They and their children provided much comfort and company to the ageing Dowager Empress. Michael, the youngest son, was a rather wild and irresponsible young man for whom the whole family felt concern. When he married Helena Pavlovna in 1824, everyone hoped for an improvement in his behaviour. Unfortunately, these anticipations were not to be realized. His brother, Constantine, had summed up his character earlier as caring 'only for sleeping and giving military service'. Less is said of Constantine, since he made only fleeting visits to see his mother and brothers. Besides, he was a regular correspondent of his sister in any case. His marriage to Joanna Grudzinska, following his divorce from Anna Feodorovna, a Saxe-Coburg princess from whom he had long been separated, is noted. Initially, it seems his nuptials were performed without prior approval by the Emperor, but a year later it seems the entire family accepted the situation. Actually, this morganatic marriage made no difference as there were no children, and even if there had been they could not have succeeded to the throne. Nicholas and his sons were in line for the succession ultimately.

Few persons aside from the intimate court circles are mentioned. The 'Dear Countess', later Princess, Lieven, is very much part of the entourage. Her general health is a frequent topic. In The Netherlands only Dr Harry and 'Bourcis', Mademoiselle de Sybourg, seem to warrant the concern of Anna Pavlovna's mother.

Of course, there are the usual polite references to the Dutch royal family, but with the exception of frequent expressions of regard for the Prince of Orange, these remarks are only incidental. Only rarely does Anna Pavlovna's relationship with her husband's family come under close scrutiny from her mother, and it is generally to admonish or to praise her for some particular act. It is evident that Maria Feodorovna regarded the unusually happy domestic existence of her youngest daughter with much pleasure. With her strong maternal sentiments she feels her grandchildren in The Netherlands, as well as those in Weimar and Russia, are very special beings.

In 1824 Anna Pavlovna made a visit to St Petersburg to see her mother and her family. It was a most happy occasion, and she and her husband were to stay in Russia for some months. There were copious tears on parting; fortunately, Anna Pavlovna was not to know that this would be the last occasion she would see her mother or her brother, the Emperor Alexander.

Alexander and his wife had been estranged for a number of years but had recently been reconciled. The imperial couple decided to spend the winter at Taganrog, in the south of Russia. The reason for this decision was to make an effort to improve the health of the Empress. She and her husband departed for the southern part of the country in late summer. The Emperor made his way more quickly because he wanted to make a tour of the Crimea. Early in November they were united in Taganrog. After only a brief illness – probably a fever caught during his tour of inspection – Alexander died on 19 November 1825. He was only forty-eight years of age.

News of his demise took some days to reach the capital. It was not until 27 November that the imperial family were informed of what had occurred. Nicholas immediately proclaimed his brother Constantine as Emperor and he took an oath of allegiance. However, when this was reported to Constantine in Warsaw, he categorically refused to accept the Crown. Apparently it had always been his intention to reject the imperial office, and this was known to his late brother. The latter had actually placed a written statement with the Holy Synod, naming Nicholas as his heir. However, this had no legal standing because of the decision made by their father unless Constantine formally gave up his rights. This had not been done. Finally, Nicholas was forced to accept the fact that his elder brother was adamant in his decision. On 14 December, Nicholas was proclaimed; what followed this series of events was very tragic.

Certain regiments led by some liberal officers and youthful idealists resisted the new Emperor's accession. Troops loyal to the latter fired on the rebels and very quickly the affair was at an end. The principal ringleaders, most of whom were members of distinguished families, were arrested, interrogated and ultimately tried for treason. Five of the conspirators were hanged, the remainder exiled to Siberia. Maria Feodorovna was convinced that these revolutionaries deserved the harshest of punishments. One of the conspirators was a Prince Volkonski, the son of a friend, but she showed no pity for him.

Life in St Petersburg soon resumed its even tenor. Maria Feodorovna's progresses from Pavlovsk to Gatchina to the Winter Palace continued as in the past, as did her visits to her charitable and educational institutions. Even the death of Elizabeth Alexievna, the widow of Alexander, in the spring of 1826, was hardly to cause a ripple in the routine. Maria Feodorovna attended Nicholas's coronation in Moscow in 1826 and was delighted to see him so happy.

In the summer of 1828, Maria Feodorovna was far from well; her general situation gave no cause for alarm and she made only the most brief allusions to her health in her correspondence. Evidently she was seriously ill and on 24 October she died. Anna Pavlovna was informed of her mother's demise immediately; the family was prostrate with grief. Alexandra, the wife of Nicholas, expressed their feelings to Anna Pavlovna. In her will, Maria Feodorovna left bequests to all of her children but favouring Michael and Maria as they were the least well provided for. Anna Pavlovna accepted her mother's decision graciously. However, she asked Constantine to give her the Murillo painting which he had inherited as it had been in the study of Pavlovsk. It was to be a particular souvenir of the past.

For Anna Pavlovna, the death of Maria Feodorovna marked the end of an age. Never again would she have such close contact with Russia. The demise of Constantine in 1831 cut the ties still further. Maria Feodorovna had guided her daughter in a judicious fashion; she had admonished her and praised her, and had made her the recipient of her maternal generosity. Truly, Anna Pavlovna could say in a letter written to Constantine, 'a new era is beginning for us and for me . . . more I think than for all the others; Mama was my refuge, my support, I could open my heart to her and she deigned to encourage me with her advice! All that is finished, so I feel so alone . . . I must pray Heaven ceaselessly to support me and to help me fulfil the duties imposed on me! . . .'

## *Note on the Method of Editing the Correspondence*

The letters were originally written in French and in the translation every effort has been made to retain the general tone and style of the Empress Maria Feodorovna. Formal salutations and conclusions have been omitted since they add little to the text. Family letters become tedious if burdened with the trappings of scholarship. Excessive footnotes, etc., make reading difficult and, consequently, following the advice of the late Sir Roger Fulford, the distinguished editor of the letters of Queen Victoria to her eldest daughter, I have seen fit not to use them. A *dramatis personae* is given to identify the principal people in the text. The Romanovs had nicknames for their children, and these have been shown. The dates on the letters are those in use in Russia at that time, i.e. using the Julian Calendar. I have provided a general introduction to the correspondence which will serve to give a brief portrait sketch of the author and her times.

# Dramatis Personae

**ALEXANDER** The eldest brother of Anna Pavlovna, often referred to in the text as 'the Emperor'. After his death in 1825 he was generally called 'Our Angel'.

**ELIZABETH ALEXIEVNA** The wife of Alexander, born Princess Louise of Baden, referred to in the letters as 'the Empress'.

**CONSTANTINE** Brother of Anna Pavlovna, Viceroy of Poland, he lived in Warsaw. Paul is his illegitmate son.

**JOANNA GRUDZINSKA, PRINCESS LOWICZ** The morganatic second wife of Constantine.

**MARIA** Sister of Anna Pavlovna and wife of Grand Duke Charles of Saxe-Weimar (referred to as Marie).

**NICHOLAS** Younger brother of Anna Pavlovna, later Emperor Nicholas I, referred to as Nix, Nikki, 'the Emperor'.

**ALEXANDRA FEODOROVNA** Wife of Nicholas, born Princess Charlotte of Prussia, referred to as Alexandrine or Sachine.

**ALEXANDER (SASHA), MARIE, OLGA (OLINE), ALEXANDRA, CONSTANTINE (COSTY)** Children of Nicholas and Alexandra.

**MICHAEL** Youngest brother of Anna Pavlovna.

**HELENA PAVLOVNA** Wife of Michael, born Princess Charlotte of Wurttemberg.

**CHARLOTTE LIEVEN** The 'dear countess', created Princess in 1826 by Nicholas I, friend and lady-in-waiting to Maria Feodorovna.

**PAUL ALEXANDROV** Called Paul, illegitimate son of Constantine, accepted by Maria Feodorovna as a member of the family.

## *The Netherlands*

**WILLIAM I** 'The King', father-in-law of Anna Pavlovna.

**WILHELMINA** 'The Queen', mother-in-law of Anna Pavlovna.

**WILLIAM** Prince of Orange, husband of Anna Pavlovna.

**WILLIAM, ALEXANDER, HENRY, ERNST, SOPHIE** Children of Anna Pavlovna.

**FREDERICK** Brother of William, Prince of Orange.

**LOUISE** Wife of Prince Frederick of The Netherlands, sister of Alexandra Feodorovna.

**MARIANNE** Sister of William, Prince of Orange.

**DR HARRY** Medical adviser to Anna Pavlovna.

# 1820

## Thursday 1 January

My blessings and best wishes to you, Dear Anne, as to William and the children. May God grant you all a happy year and reunite us one day. The cold has lessened somewhat so that today was perfect. Alexandrine and D— had a wonderful time and was delighted at the sight of the supper room. We've added to the number of crystals. I'm a little tired tonight, dear Anne, and will end these lines by sending you a fond kiss and my dear love.

## 4 January

The courier who was supposed to leave five days ago hasn't left yet so I'm taking advantage of this chance to send you my letter of congratulations on this special day. I just returned from mass where I prayed for you with all my heart. May God keep and bless you. Your letter in today's mail worried me since your fever has returned. I believe, my dear child, that all these indispositions are caused by your condition. You would experience the same symptoms in Brussels as you do at The Hague and I really don't see the climate as the only cause, but certainly it worries me a lot.

## Tuesday 6 January

I hope to be able to send you my cheque for 10,000 roubles tomorrow but I won't send you my gift, meant for both your celebration days combined until February. I have had a chain of topaz' made up for you. Half is for this feast and the other will be for the one in February but I don't want to send it until the whole necklace is ready. I hope it will please you. I know it's your favourite stone and William's too. All the family congratulate you wholeheartedly and send kisses, as does the good Countess. The military parade to mark the day did not take place though because it was minus twenty-three. Tonight it is minus twenty-five. This winter is frightfully harsh. I can't remember one with such unrelieved cold. Good night my dearest.

## *Wednesday 7 January*

It would be cruel if your indisposition were caused by the climate. You've got to live there, dear child, so you must try by all means to get used to it. This will require taking many precautions and great care but you will eventually succeed. How chagrined the Dutch people would be if they noticed that you felt that way. They expect to feel loved and appreciated because they have first claim to your loyalty. Both the degree and the length of their attachment to the House of Orange demand it. So you must convince them that you are happy in their country and in their company. I hope and pray that God will strengthen your health and give you the courage necessary to withstand the demands of the climate. It will enhance your image in the eyes of the nation. I am sending you, dear child, a bonnet which I had embroidered here for you as a copy of one of mine which I had in Brussels and which you admired. It's considered to be even better embroidered than the white one. Wear it often in memory of me. It might be useful during your lying-in. You will be happy to hear that today for the first time our dear Michael assisted in the work of our dear Emperor. This ought to have had a salutory effect on his tendency to be self-centred.

## *Thursday 8 January*

Our entertainment yesterday was very successful, dear Annette. The voice of La Burgundi goes straight to the heart. She sings alto and has a magnificent voice which is charming, in the best style of Italian singing without that ever lasting warbling which I do not like. The Emperor was at the performance and was pleased with the singer.

## *11 January*

Finally my dear child I received a letter from William which tells me that you are pregnant. I rejoice with all my heart for it increases your happiness, his and certainly will make you even more dear to your new country. He also reassures me that you are feeling well.

## St Petersburg
### *15 January*

Your last letter, darling Annette, seriously worries me. I see you so unhappy about your health that you even show enough lack of interest in living which in all counts should be far from your mind. Your condition naturally brings on its own miseries, revulsion, weakness, even prostration. But as you quite rightly said during your first pregnancy, this suffering was dear to you as it earned you the happiness of motherhood. Your condition sometimes brings such a state but you must treat it as an enemy of your peace of mind, of your happiness, of William's, the children's, ours and dispel it by force of reason and by determined will power. The last mail but one brought me a letter from William which tells me that your health is good. I suppose, therefore, that your sensations are due both to your conditions and to a nervous temperament for which air and amusements are essential. I implore you therefore my darling Annette, to be brave and to seek in reflection, occupation, exercise, and a little amusement the remedy for the ills inseparable from your state. Above all my good Anne, you will find comfort in reasoning with yourself. In telling yourself that God is with you and requires you to place complete trust in His tenderness. That belief will then be your help, even in your worst moments. Oh how I wish I could fly to you and talk to you. I am sure that after an hour of conversation, my Annette would reject all ideas of collapse, would give herself entirely to the joy of being a happy wife, mother, daughter, sister and would reproach herself for this moment of weakness. I must add that as spring approaches a thousand pleasant distractions await you and the possibility of getting a lot of exercise will do you good.

### *29 January*

A masquerade yesterday was very successful, darling Anne, and we had an amusing time. There were some beautiful costumes, but Alexandrine was without any doubt the most beautiful of all, dressed as Roxanne, wife of Alexander. It suited her marvellously. There were scenes from comedy, singing, a parade of dear little children, tableau, it was well done and really pleased the invited public. I went home at 2:00 a.m. The room was decorated with real flowers which they will scarcely credit at The Hague. In between the pillars they had decorated with leaves; then there were the great vases filled with flowers – it was truly beautiful.

### *4 February*

I congratulate you with all my heart, dearest friend, on the Feast Day of our dear Marie. You love her so tenderly that this day is a day of rejoicing for you as much as it is for me. I wanted to celebrate the day with a ball but as we were returning from Mass a courier brought us the news of the death of the King of England so out of consideration for the King and his nation I had to cancel the ball. I wrote you yesterday by courier which is why this letter has only a day's news in it.

### *Friday 6 February*

I have received your letters, my dear Anne, and thank God you are better. But how sad your news of the flooding is. The losses are terrible. God willing that at least there be no loss of life. I hope you will give me all the details. How our dear William must suffer from these misfortunes.

### *Monday 19 February*

We are terribly shocked by the assassination of the Duke de Berri, dear Anne and you can imagine the horror and fear that this event causes us. It's impossible to think of a family as unfortunate as that of the Bourbons. I'll admit to you that I can't stop thinking of the Duchesse d'Angoulême and the unhappy young widow. How I thank God, dear Anne for having prevented your marriage to this poor Duke de Berri. How providence has looked after you. I am eternally grateful for all these blessings.

### *Saturday 20 February*

My letter to you was just put aside to continue later as was Marie's when they brought us three issues of the *Journal des Débats* which contained the details of the assassination of the Duke de Berri. I began to read and couldn't put the papers down until I had finished them which took me until 2:00 in the morning by which time my eyes refused to do any more work.

Dear child. How fortunate, dear child, that the damage caused by the floods won't be as serious as we had feared. I note with pleasure, dear child, all the aid flowing in from the provinces for these victims. The people will bless you, my dear, for doing good and working for the poor as you do.

### *Sunday 22 February*

We heard Mass at the institute, dear child, and the Emperor and Empress took pleasure in seeing the children. Tomorrow they are going to sing the pieces they performed for the examination and I am sure that the Emperor will be pleased.

### *Friday 27 February*

I see that you have got rid of your infection, dear child, and I am very glad. I know from experience these abcesses in the mouth, they make you suffer death and martyrdom and unfortunately when you are pregnant you are susceptible to them. The assassination of the Duke de Berri strikes you with the same anguish and terror as ourselves. It certainly preys on the imagination. I could also see William when he got the news and have a vivid idea of his indignation.

### *Monday 1 March*

I am very happy to know that the losses of the inhabitants is not as bad as originally expected but I fear that those houses that were soaked in water are dangerous to the health of the good people that live in them. I am pleased to know that the Queen is happy with the amethyst jewellery which she had made here for herself and I am sure it suits her splendidly. I am afraid that she has completely forgotten me because I have received neither an answer to my letter nor a friendly message through you, dear child. However, I remain sincerely fond of her. The beginning of this year has been blighted by two horrible political murders inspired, I believe, by the same atrocious ideas as those belonging to that criminal group who delight in evil doing.

### *Saturday 13 March*

I am very pleased that you are satisfied with your new cantor who I agree does have a charming voice and who is also a good musician. Anybody who has a great love of music must be delighted with our Lentan Masses. One never tires of them. Tell me, my dear Anne, is your chapel at The Hague in the same style as the one in Brussels which I thought was so attractive?

## Monday 15 March

I spent my morning at the community [Smolny], dear child, where I attended a minor examination then I went to the hospital and then I went to hug my dear grandchildren who are quite delightful. The little girl is getting much prettier and will be as pretty as her mother. She is very — and already cherishes her father who gives her a lot of attention and who is much amused by her. He truly loves her. As for the little boy, he's an angel and the best child possible. May God keep them both. I only wish they could play with your children.

## Wednesday 17 March

The accounts of the new disasters caused by the hurricane and flooding greatly distress me. It's frightful how this year's harsh winter has caused such damage throughout Europe. I can well imagine, dear Annette, how saddened you must be to know of such suffering among your people. But I am sure you do all you can and that they bless you for it.

## Tuesday evening 23 March

Are you showing yet, dear child and do you still expect to have a baby girl? That's what I am hoping for you as you already have the great joy of having two sons. Fathers welcome daughters. Nick is crazy over his little girl who in fact is a little angel, pretty as a picture, very gay and very lively.

## Holy Thursday 25 March

Don't you think, dear Annette that you were very lucky in avoiding the Spanish marriage? It's obvious that heaven is watching over you since both France and Spain would have brought you misery. I am very sorry for the poor young Queen of Spain. Right after her arrival there she had to face all this revolutionary activity which is so dangerous. What does William say about everything that is happening there and about the disastrous example which the Spanish army is giving to Europe?

### Easter Tuesday 30 March

You are doing a good deed in caring for the daughter of your Master of the Horse. Believe me, you gather treasure for your own children in extending your kindness to such unfortunate youngsters. Her father will bless your name a thousand times a day. Thank you dear child for the rosebushes and the dahlias and I hope they will do well. I did not want to tell you dear Annette, that our dear Emperor had to keep to his room for a few days with a boil on his chin. It appeared on Good Friday and as it even prevented the Emperor from doing his beard, he could not make a public appearance on Easter Sunday, even though he felt perfectly well. It's dried up now and he will be going out tomorrow which is why I feel I can tell you about it now that we are not worried anymore. Thank God there was no need to be as his health is generally good. He felt only a little pain on Friday and on Saturday it was all better. I am very obliged to you dear child for your last letter which assures me that you are well. I see dear Annette that you are still pleased with your new cantor and that your daily service attracts people to your chapel. Certainly our church music is exceptionally beautiful.

### Saturday 3 April

I hope that you are now enjoying, dear child, all the first beauties of spring and that you will soon be moving to your country place where you will be able to go out as you like. I expect that you will have your baby there as before, especially as you expect it in June. It seems to me to be essential that your lying-in be in the country where you will recover sooner and get back your strength. I speak from experience having always felt better myself when my children were born at Czarskoeselo. I am sure that the good Queen will be of the same opinion especially since you have already established the precedent and there's no reason for it not being so.

### Tuesday 6 April

I hope that you are already gathering violets and that soon dear Annette you will be telling me that you are on your way to the country.

## *Friday 9 April*

I am all yours, my dear girl. I can finally answer your long very good letter. First, let me thank you for your confidence in me which I deeply value. I have received the package containing your second will and it's in safe keeping as you have asked and, thank God, I won't be the executor. According to the natural order, I will precede you, I hope by some fifty years. However, it is secure in my safe addressed to the Emperor. You tell me to burn, to nullify the first will. I admit that I couldn't resolve myself to do it, my dear child and I am sending it to you under separate cover. It is in the same wrapping that you put on it at Brussels where I wrote in your presence a few lines with the place and date. I didn't want to destroy them either in case you might want to keep your mother's words. I see that your affairs are in good state, my dear child, as since you have been married you have already been able to set aside a little. At the same time you devote yourself to the needs of your court, extending your charity and helping the poor as much as you can. You are behaving as a wise wife and a provident mother. If you go on this way you will be a rich and powerful lady but I am sure you will always regard the duty to be as charitable as possible to be one of your first obligations. I see dear child by your letter that if unfortunately the King's heart towards you two hasn't changed for the better, at least appearances are observed and that William's wise conduct has earned him respect for his opinions. The latest gazettes have announced that the new budget will pass and that William was involved in it. I rejoice in the thought that this success will be due to his careful way and his good management. He is calm, respectful, even tempered, deferential and frank at the same time which will gain for him the esteem of his father and the love and confidence of his subjects. I am happy that you see people regularly. William will win the love of the Dutch as well as that of the Flemish by his behaviour and the equal treatment that you give to The Hague and to Brussels will prove to both countries that you feel at home with them and that you are equally happy to be with people from either country. It will be an important point won. You have already seen my dear girl in my letters sent by the mail that I spoke of your lying-in and my wish that you deliver in the country, citing my own example. I hope that you will use that letter, if necessary, but I don't suppose the King will put restrictions on your third delivery that he didn't find necessary to put on the second. I am glad to see that the Queen is still a good and tender mother to you. Indeed I am sure that her behaviour to you won't change because it is not in her character. But then tell me my child, why hasn't she answered my last letter written for her birthday? I must suppose that the letter was lost. She knows that I am sincerely fond of her. She has also demonstrated friendship for me. Therefore I don't know how to interpret this silence. She doesn't even send a message by you. How tiresome it is that little Marianne is so badly brought up. I will admit that I thought her companions were poorly chosen. Her governess may well be a good and excellent woman but she doesn't seem to me to be the right person to raise a young princess. Her diet also astonishes me and may adversely affect her health. It's too bad that she should be so spoiled for it seemed to me that she was bright. All opinions agree as to Prince Frederick who was very well thought of during the trips he made last year. According to my assessment which I made of him in Brussels, what you tell me of him, dear Annette and the general good opinion of him, I am convinced he will bring happiness to the person he marries. Indeed I will admit to you, dear Annette that it would give us considerable pleasure if he should choose my niece Marie, daughter of my brother Alexander. By all reports she is a pretty and likeable girl, good character, an excellent child. She has a natural grace, a friendly nature and is an excellent musician. She has a very unassuming manner as well so that she can't help but please. I will even tell you that this marriage would give as much pleasure to the Emperor as to myself as he honours my sister-in-law with his friendship and includes the dear girl who we are all fond of. She'll spend the summer in Germany again because her mother has to take waters either at Carlsbad or at Baden near Carlsbad so that the Prince who has I believe already seen her once in Vienna could see her again this summer. If you can advance this marriage you would be doing me a real service for which the Emperor and I would thank you very warmly. It's unlikely that once the Prince evidences a desire to settle down he should be left without an establishment of his own. Why would his father put off this business for the state to do after his death? It seems to depend on the Prince's wish to get married. If he decides for it then the establishment must follow. Do your best, dear child, to arrange this union. You know how to respect my confidence. The case of the unhappy Princess of Orange touches me deeply. To suffer and to suffer at the hands of a son must be worse than dying. You do well my dear child to increase the respectful attentions you pay her. Love her as a daughter would and your filial devotion will bless you and your children with happiness. How abused the poor woman must feel. Does she begin to receive a few visitors? I am very glad dear child to know you are so pleased with your entourage. Madame de Fagel seemed to me to be a very distinguished person and certainly if heaven grants you a daughter I think you would do well to entrust the little one to her care. I admit that I hope you will have a girl as you already have two sons, a little girl would be for your personal happiness. But I hope she will be very pretty and in every way the equal of your two charming boys who I send my love to. I see the older boy no longer remembers me. As for the younger one who was still nursing, he couldn't have any memory of my existence. May God grant me the happiness of seeing them one day. Unfortunately I don't have much hope. I see you're happy with your country place at Soestdijk. I'd really like to know your places at The Hague and beg you to draw for me, even if it be in pencil, the position of your rooms, their use so that I can imagine myself in your environment. I see that you've taken up your drawing again which pleases me enormously. It was cruel to neglect such a charming talent. I am sure that you will take all your old delight in it.

### Tuesday 13 April

Poor darling. Your husband's gone to Brussels, the Court and your family to Amsterdam and you are left all alone. How I wish that I could come and keep you company. I would be so happy if it were possible. Tell me, why did William leave you at the same time as the Queen had to be away? Certainly since he did it must have been unavoidable.

### Tuesday 22 April

Dear child. We have received the news of the marriage of the King of Wurttemburg, so our poor Catherine is replaced in the heart of her husband and her children have a second mother. They say though that she is sweet, good and lovable so I hope she will make the King and his children happy. This news will affect you as it does me. It brings our loss so vividly to mind.

### Monday 3 May

I have enjoyed such a beautiful day today, dear Annette and I had the pleasure of gathering violets. There are a lot this spring and the perfume is delicious. Our dear Emperor dined at my place. He looked very well and Gatchina greatly pleased him. I haven't heard a nightingale yet. . . . Farewell my dear.

### Tuesday 4 May

It seems to me that dear Alexander is becoming a bit of a favourite and that poor William is left out. I'll stay loyal to him though because I thought he was a delightful child and very good for his age. I am glad that your figure is changing dear child. It's as nature ordains and for the love of God don't corset yourself in.

### Friday 21 May

I have returned from Czarskoeselo where I dined with the Emperor. That is, we celebrated the feast of the day together after attending Mass. They are already working on the building and the roof is being put on. It's advancing rapidly and we expect that the main part of the damage will be fixed by the winter. I will be very happy. It was so sad to see the beautiful château in that condition. The weather was rainy last night and this morning too but the vegetation has benefited. It's superb. My garden is brimming with flowers. I still want, dear child, the seeds which you are keeping for me. They will not spoil.

### Pavlovsk
### 26 May

It was a gorgeous day so I went out both morning and evening. Everything near your pavilion looks charming. The greenery is so fresh that it delights and rests the eyes. The famous Catelani has arrived and is giving her first concert in town so that everybody has gone to hear her. I am sure she will be a big success.

### Saturday 29 May

Tell me dear Annette, won't you go to Spa after the baby is born? The waters are so strengthening, they are sure to do you good. When will the Queen arrive to stay with you? Won't Sybourg come for your lying-in? All I can think of is your delivery. God willing you will have as easy a time as possible.

## *15 June*

I have just read your letter with the sad news of the death of the Princess of Orange and I am so, so sorry. I thank God that you too appreciated her, especially lately and will sincerely mourn her. Unfortunately her corpulence made a sudden death likely and I am also sure that the death of her daughter hastened her own.

## *16 June*

Darling Annette. How I embrace you. How I congratulate you a thousand and a thousand times on your safe delivery. Just after dinner the courier arrived at the chargé d'affaires and Count Nesselrode immediately sent me my letters. William is very happy with his third little son and you will be as well. Everybody is congratulating me, dear Annette. The Emperor came to see me, your three brothers left the troops to come and congratulate me. Everybody surrounded me with that tenderness which we have for each other. Alexandrine was also thrilled with the news. Her brother Prince Charles arrived today which makes her very happy.

## *Friday 2 July*

A thousand good wishes to your three dear little boys. How I wish I could see you all. The two oldest are already quite big. What languages do they speak? The Emperor left us to go to Czarskoeselo. He and your other brothers and sisters send tender regards as does the dear Countess. May God keep you dear child. Think often of your old mama who loves you very much.

## Pavlovsk
## *7 July*

Our dear Emperor leaves us the day after tomorrow to make his grand tour of Russia and to get to Warsaw by August 15th where he will stay for the 6 weeks of the Diet. He will be back, God willing on October the 14th. It's still hard to see him go. Our dear Nicky is a dear husband. It is impossible to be more careful, more attentive than he is of his wife. He looks after her as well as the most devoted maid-in-waiting. I bless God for their happiness for it couldn't be more complete. Michael is as good as ever. I hope he will one day find domestic happiness but unfortunately the word on available princesses is that there's very little hope of finding one who's worthy of him. This is a great sorrow to me.

## *Sunday 11 July*

Darling Annette. I couldn't write to you yesterday. You'll imagine what my day was like when you know that yesterday at 5:05 our dear Alexandrine was delivered safely and easily of a baby girl, already two weeks dead.

## *Monday 12 July*

Alexandrine was prepared for the loss of her child by the lack of movement and had already cried many tears. But she listened to our tender consolations and resigned herself to wait. Since her delivery left her no more grounds for hope, she wept again. We reminded her that we could all thank God that he protected her from such obvious danger, and that we should therefore be grateful and resigned. She made the sign of the cross and allowed herself no further lament. She has behaved with great sweetness. God will reward her by blessing her children and by granting her yet others.

## *Saturday 17 July*

You will have seen in the gazettes that Constantine was married to a maid-of-honour. The Emperor has issued a law which I sent you nullifying the consequences that the union could have. Constantine wrote me after the wedding to ask my forgiveness and to tell me all the reasons which prompted him to get married and to say that he had contracted this marriage in part so that his descendants would not compete with Nicholas' line. That seems to be indeed his intention. His wife will carry the name of Princess of a region which the Emperor will give to Constantine and will enjoy no other royal prerogative. *I don't mention her by name in any of my letters* and he observes the same silence in all those he writes to me with exception of the one in which he announced his marriage and asked my forgiveness. You know, dear Annette, that all this has hurt me and distressed me but fortunately the possible regrettable implications of the union have been nullified. As well he has broken off a shameful liaison that was damaging him in the public opinion. The woman he has married is by all accounts a good person. Her appearance is agreeable and gentle. Has your brother written to you about this, my dear child? All your brothers are very well. Nicky is devoting himself to his wife and watches over her and cares for her with touching zeal. He is her nurse, spends the nights still dressed, lying on a mattress near her. Indeed it would be impossible to do more or to see a couple more perfectly in love. May heaven preserve them each for the other. Their children are charming. The little boy prays a lot and is changing daily. He's a most delightful child. The little girl is also charming, a delightful little doll full of pretty ways. She is beginning to crawl. She wants to talk but doesn't have any teeth yet. Michael is also well and very busy with his army work. He's doing well. I am very sorry to see so little chance of future happiness for him because of the total lack of Princesses. There's really a complete dearth of suitable girls. I confess I don't know what's going to happen to him. He's almost 23 and he needs to be happily married. We'll have to trust in God to watch over him. Did the Princess of Orange leave a will and will it be respected? Why is she buried at Het Loo, not with her daughter? Didn't she have any presentiment of her death? How long will the mourning period be? How is the King's health? Has he recovered and is the Queen well? What is Marianne doing and is she improving? Everything you tell me about Prince Frederick is contrary to the opinion I had of him. He seemed to me to be very good natured, very stable. They say he's marrying Princess Marie of Hesse in which case he'll have a charming wife. I will always miss her. She was very pleasant and had a pronounced resemblance to our Alexandrine. I was very glad, my dear, to see that your child would be baptized in the country as I know that will please you. Is the King coming? It seems that those two weeks premature haven't done the baby any harm but why does the obstetrician think you delivered early? I suppose that the shock of the death of the Princess of Orange was the cause. I am sure my dear that the waters of the Spa and the effervescent baths will do you good. Nicholas is very jealous of William for having three sons. I wanted more sons for him too but God's will be done. The Grand Duchess will need time and medical resources to strengthen her health and her nerves. Nicholas is already distracted at the abstinence he must observe, but all the doctors say that the constitution of the Grand Duchess demands some rest after those close pregnancies. She didn't even have one period between Marie's birth and the pregnancy with the dead baby, and that's why she lost so much blood which has weakened her and caused the poor tone of her skin. She was terribly swollen but thank God that has passed. Nicholas and Alexandrine will take a trip to Berlin this autumn. They were going to go in the spring but Alexandrine's condition prevented it. I think they will be absent six months and you will think of me and pray for me. When I was at *Mont Pléasire* I threw a stone into the sea for you. I picked up another and sent it to the shop to have it polished and the date engraved on it. I will send it to you as a paper weight. Then I went to the mill which isn't producing pretty things yet. Next year it will, they say. I took three stones for tokens from there too and will send them to you. Give one to William. I wanted to send two little swords like the one I gave Alexander to your two sons but the supplier didn't have any more. You will get them, though, as soon as possible.

## 27 July

I congratulate you my dear on having finished your lying-in period and on the baptism of the dear child. How I wish I could have been present at that ceremony. It must have been very touching and it was a good idea to follow the customs of the country. It is necessary to respect such customs, they are the ties that unite a country and so really you have no choice.

## 7 August

Our dear Alexander has sent me good reports my dear from Tilburg dated July 31st. He's travelling very comfortably and is well satisfied with his troops. In seven days he will arrive in Warsaw after quite a considerable journey. I will be very happy to know when he's safely there. At least he won't be travelling still further away from us. The Empress returned to Oranienbaum today. I was her guest at Czarskoeselo.

## 10 August

It's very sweet to know that I am as dear to you as even I could wish. Thank you for the bulbs you sent me for my birthday. I have always heard that the trip that William has just made to the northern provinces must be very interesting. I find your penmanship a bit shaky so what's the matter and what are these accidents which happened during your pregnancy that you did not want to tell me about? I have told you quite clearly that I want to know all details. The truth is always more reassuring. Alexandrine is all right, very well. What do you mean then dear Annette that you are indisposed. I hope that its only the return of a certain period that tires you so and gives you depression and cramps. However, I am anxiously awaiting your next letter telling me that you are better. The strengthening baths should do you a lot of good and so would the diet. I am grateful to dear William for finishing your letter and I am very touched by his kindness. He speaks of you my dear in such tender terms that I am doubly happy. You must look after yourself and take pains to regain your health. Alexandrine is well and is visibly recovering.

### *25 August*

Your letter reassured me a great deal, darling Annette since Dr Harry allows you to leave for your trip. I have a great deal of faith in the waters of Spa which will strengthen you and as you spend the winter in a warmer climate I expect that you will make a complete recovery. We've had charming weather. I've made the Grand Tour out and about. Pavlovsk is just beautiful and pleases everybody. Good night dear Annette.

### *Thursday 26 August*

We've been very interested in the eclipse, dear child, which we saw perfectly from here as the sky was quite clear. It must have been total where you are and maybe you were watching it at the same time as us. I went out on horseback this morning and dined at Madame de Clerhoff's residence. I am sure you will remember her wonderful dinners and the excellent mushroom dishes she serves.

### St Petersburg
### *29 August*

Let me congratulate you, darling Annette on the dear Emperor's birthday. May God keep him for our happiness and indeed for that of all Europe. May the supreme being protect his sacred person from all harm and grant him a full measure of happiness.

## *Tuesday 31 August*

Dear Annette, so you've arrived at Spa. I trust the waters will cure you and I am sure, my dear child, that a little weakness of the nerves accounts for a great deal of your trouble. Moderate exercise, tonics and some amusement will dispel these lingering effects of giving birth. I am going to speak to old Crichton about your condition. I wish that Harry's reports gave adequate details but I will tell him what I know. I would very much like Harry to consult Crichton about you. He's soon going to leave us and Harry could write to him in Paris so that he will be given the letter when he arrives. As he's known you from childhood, his advice will be useful. He himself is slowly recovering from a serious illness having suffered an inflammation of the liver.

## *6 September*

I dined today with Count Kotschoubey whose daughter was married last Friday to Baron Stroganoff, son of our envoy to Constantinople. You will remember the father and the mother who's an excellent person and who I sometimes see at Pavlovsk. Count Kotschoubey's house is at Czarskoeselo, built at the far end of the garden and, therefore, facing the garden with a façade towards the main road. It's one of the prettiest houses I've ever seen and it's most pleasantly situated. Nicky and Alexandrine have gone to town to pack for their long trip. Prince Charles left us last night with obvious regret. He'll go by Smolensk and Grodno on his way to Berlin.

## *Wednesday 7 September*

I had the great joy of receiving good news from my dear Emperor dated the 30th from Warsaw. His feast day was celebrated there by a superb ball given by the Viceroy. The Diet was to open the following day. The people of Warsaw are so happy to see the dear Emperor. He is adored there as he well deserves to be. I am trusting that you want to hear the news I have from the

Emperor even though I expect the public news has already informed you of the facts. What are you doing, dear Annette? Is the Spa water doing you good?

## *Monday 20 September*

Dear Annette. Like me you will have thought of your dear affectionate father today and our prayers for him are joined. I spent the day in retreat so I have nothing interesting to tell you. Good night dear child.

## *Wednesday 22 September*

How pleased I am darling child to see that your health allows you to receive people and even give luncheons. Though you are not dancing yet, that will come. I am very happy that Prince Frederick comes to see you. He's a very likeable young man, distinguished in character and mind. Please give him my regards. Has anything yet been decided about his future? The garden at Gatchina seems to me to be as beautiful as ever with many autumn flowers still blooming. By the way, my fine lady, you told me that for July 29th you were sending me a gift of flowers but here we are at the end of the sailing season for the year and I haven't received them. So I beg you, my dear child, to inquire where the parcel ended up.

## *Thursday 23 September*

I am writing to you to the beating of drums, singing and the noise of my grandchildren's games. What a pleasure to see them so gay and so happy and so full of life. God grant it will always be so. I am already so used to this commotion that it doesn't interfere with my activities.

## *Friday 1 October*

So dear Annette, from what I've read, William was summoned to The Hague. I thought he might take a trip to see the Emperor. Your letter confirms it. I am sure William is very happy with this evidence of the King's confidence in him and the chance of seeing our dear Emperor. Today my children, Nick and Alexandrine arrived in Berlin. Great joy.

### *2 October*

As I figure it, William will be close to his reunion with our dear Emperor. How patiently you will be awaiting his return dear Annette. I am afraid the separation will seem long to you but your dear children will keep you busy and be your conservation. How happy Marie will be to see William again and how sorry I am that I can't hope for this happiness for myself.

### *Monday 25 October*

They brought 25 baskets of roses to my address Sa Majesté Imperiale. I haven't had any information about a Dutch ship. You have sent me no message or notice of the flowers being sent but I do remember that you wrote to me when you saw the beautiful display of your roses in the country and said that you would give them to me and that you wanted to send me some. I suppose therefore that it's an *extraordinary gift* from you and send you my fondest thanks. It shows love for both me and Pavlovsk to thus *rosify* me. I embrace you with all my heart for the gift and only beg you to notify me next time you send me something as sometimes in spite of it being sent to my address I worry that I might be appropriating what belongs to someone else.

### *Friday 27 October*

The King and Queen are very kind in inviting you to come and dine when you like at the palace and that must please you. Certainly these days the greatest possible family unity is most important and discourages evil wishers.

### *Thursday 28 October*

I am often with you in imagination, dear Annette, in your pretty apartments and seeing myself with you in the blue drawing room. Tell me, dear child, are there many flowers in your orangerie? Do you often go there? When do you use the rooms downstairs? I read the speech which the King gave at the opening of the Estates General and was delighted to see that our own dear Emperor had used his influence for the King. Please tell the Queen of my faithful regard for her. Is she still interested in painting?

### *Saturday 30 October*

Tell me, dear child if the family gathering still takes place in the same room and if the after dinner activities are the same? How empty the family salon must appear after the deaths of the Duchess of Brunswick and the Dowager Princess. Does the Queen still receive her little group in the evening or has the custom changed? My compliments to your ladies, the Queen's ladies and all your entourage. Warmest regards to Princess Frederick whose constant friendship to you and William delights me as it must bring mutual happiness to all of you.

### *Monday 8 November*

Salutations, dear Annette, on Michael's birthday which reminds me most pleasantly of when I was in Brussels. It was the day before my departure and I could still see all the events of the day, the Mass, visits, dinner with the King, Catelani singing, waiting for the Emperor, the long session in the evening. It seems to me that I am still there with you. My heart certainly is.

### *Friday 12 November*

I have received good news from Troppau. Marie's arrived there and she and the Emperor were so happy to see each other. I can understand why. I have just had your dear letter telling me of William's iminent return and I rejoice in your happiness. Certainly the joy of a happy marriage is the greatest in the world and heaven has granted it to you. I congratulate you on the King's gift. It is very good of him and must have pleased you. Without doubt, dear Annette, you must be the Princess with the richest and most extensive collection of lace because you are so conveniently close to the source. It's a beautiful luxury and very noble. The Spanish chargé d'affaires gave me your dear letter in the package which came with it. A thousand thanks for them both. I intend to send an answer by the first courier. Thank you for the charming work basket but especially for the portrait of the black poodle. I seem to see again your superb little William playing with him and the memory warms my heart.

### *Tuesday 30 November*

Thanks for your letter dear Annette. I am sorry to see that you are suffering from the fatigue of the Queen's birthday celebrations. It could also be, my child, that you are no longer used to dancing and that you overdid it. When you are feeling more up to it you will get your old strength back and you will enjoy dancing again. You are so good at it that it will please William if you don't neglect it, at least when your health permits. Is the society of Brussels as animated as it was during your last day there, dear child? And are you and William increasing the pleasures of the season as you should by contributing your share to the entertainments? I had news from Nicholas who was leaving that evening for Troppau which made him very happy. Alexandrine is well and should completely recover. This takes a great weight from my heart.

## Tuesday 7 December

The cold or rather the thick fog keeps me indoors. It is freezing and even though the sun can be seen at noon it never quite breaks through. I see by your letter of today, my dear child, that you are enjoying balmy spring temperatures. What a wonderful country and what a charming climate. I think that it is without doubt the greatest of blessings to live in such a climate. It permits you to enjoy fresh air without being afraid of having your ears frozen off.

## 9 December

I was very happy to receive some letters from the Emperor which told me of Nicholas' arrival. And Nick for his part told me how happy he was to see his brother and find this best and most affectionate of brothers in very good health. Marie is also very happy to see Nicholas again and finds him more self assured and imposing than he used to be. Nicholas tells me about Marie's plumpness and how well she looks. I wish you too, dear Annette, have been able to somehow cross over the distance between you and our dear Alexander. However, we can trust that this pleasure is still to come and will include us. Perhaps we'll see you, William and your oldest son here. So be it.

## Saturday 10 December

Thank God that you escaped the skin disease 'erisyphylis' because that's one of those maladies which keeps coming back. I think my dear that you are counting too much on the beautiful weather and that you are not dressing warmly enough when you go out. In spite of the mild temperature you have to remember that it's winter and dress accordingly.

## *Wednesday 15 December*

I read the gazettes today, my dear child, and I saw that William's birthday was celebrated in Brussels and what the King gave him as a gift but they didn't say a word about Marianne's illness. They mentioned also that you were indisposed. I hope therefore that the dear girl is better and that all danger has passed. God will it.

## *Monday 20 December*

Many many thanks for the flowers that you sent me. They're beautiful. I must also thank you on behalf of the Countess de Lieven for the bonnet and the Countess de Lietta[?] for the hat which she thinks is charming and which indeed is. The flowers are very natural looking. They are very much to my taste which hasn't changed.

## *Sunday 26 December*

We have received some good news from our dear Emperor. It looks as though with the help and mercy of God the eruption of pus will heal. The King of Naples has embarked at Livorno and will go to Laibach which the Emperor has just left. People owe a great deal to Alexander. May God keep him and bless everything he does. I hope to hear soon that your poor little sister-in-law is better.

# *1821*

## *Tuesday 4 January*

Dear Annette. I couldn't sleep last night for worrying about you and William. I see very well by the letters from both of you that you wanted to spare me and that you haven't given me a full account of the event. However, you also sent me a letter from Chernichef for his sister so I asked her to tell me anything that related to the fire. That's how I learned what really happened. That they escaped down a ladder which William had placed for them. All sorts of other details but written in a confused way as is quite natural after such a fright. Also the chargé d'affaires gave to the Countess for me a dispatch from the minister which gave me a few more details, none of which yet satisfies me. Chernichef writes that you smelled the smoke at 4:00 in the morning and that you had your bed moved into another room but didn't William even suspect that the smoke was extraordinary, and did he also have his bed moved? When did William realize that there was a fire? Were you together when you found out? How did you get out of the house? Which stairway? And the children up on the third floor, were they warned at the same time as you? Weren't you frantic about your darlings up on another storey? And why wasn't William warned about the fire earlier? Tell me, dear Annette, how did you manage to lose your diamonds? Weren't they all closed in the same case or were they scattered all over in different places? That's never wise. Chernichef says that the pearls were thrown out through the window. Were you able to save your bank notes from the Lombards? As for that, if some were lost we could at least replace them after going through the requisite formalities. I don't understand though why your diamonds weren't among the first things saved. B— writes to Golitzene that he saved the amethyst and the golden holy vessels. Monsieur de Fagel writes that most of the silver was saved and even some furniture. So how could they possibly have left the diamonds, my dear Annette? That was among the most valuable things you had to lose. As for the rest, I expect they will search the rubble most carefully so that you will recover most of them and the diamonds won't have been damaged but the coloured gems will be spoiled. Obviously they will try to locate the diamonds, the silver and any gold but the vermilion silver dresser sets and the gold breakfast service are gone, I suppose or were they at The Hague? I have heard that poor Madame Sybourg lost everything except for one medal and that your two ladies-in-waiting and your other servants also lost everything. All this is certainly hard to accept but you must come to balance the losses with the great blessing of seeing everything safe. Tell me everything that happened. The mail hasn't brought me any of your letters. I hope to receive some on Friday and I am waiting for them most impatiently. In the meantime I have been working on your behalf. Here are the money orders for the interest on your dowry as well as the tri-annual payment of your pension from September 1820. Gourief was kind enough to include the pension from these three months as well even though it is not due until the end of the trimester. I took it on myself to ask the cabinet for some beautiful sables for you, a big coat. I am looking after a few other things. I will send you, my darling, a lovely long hooded pelisse of sable and other clothing. I will send it all to you by courier when the church is completed. I am anxious that my choices please you and fear, though that St Petersburg elegance isn't up to the standards of De Berri. But I am sending you the most beautiful things I could find, my dear daughter. I repeat, that if the police are extremely careful and sift the ashes and the rubble you are sure to recover many of your diamonds. The Queen must have been very frightened. I am sorry too that the big council room burned. In fact the whole catastrophe upsets me a great deal. Where will you all live and is the Estate's General responsible or the King for rebuilding? Please give me all these details, my dear. Tell me also if you've lost the busts and portraits of the family. Did William manage to save his beautiful painting and did you save your letters? Did your school books and your library burn? Darling Annette, I wish I could be with you to console and comfort you.

### Saturday 8 January

I was very interested in the news of the fire in the Hamburg gazettes. Is it true that it was the neighbour across the street, a Head of Department who raised the alarm? They gave the name of someone who they said had saved your jewellery. So was it true that the only gems you lost were those you were wearing the previous day? What did you lose? They said also that you are living in the townhouse of Messiers de C—, is that true?

### *Tuesday 11 January*

Tell me if you have recovered the diamonds. I was astonished my dear child to see that William has bought a house. I thought you were housed at the expense of the state and that therefore it would be the state which would be responsible for providing new accommodation. How strange that it should be arranged that way. Let me know my dear child if you want any Russian books as I suppose you will have lost them. Send me a list of what you want. Michael gives me a very good report of Monsieur d'Oviat's[?] house and tells me that the reception rooms are larger than in your previous house and very handsome. I am delighted that you are still in the neighbourhood of the park. If by any chance you still have any plans of the charming house that burned, copy them for me. I will always remember it.

### *Friday 14 January*

I have received your wonderful long letter, my dear child and thank you for it. It enlightens me somewhat on events as reported by the gazettes but not entirely. First, thank heaven that you are all right and so are your husband and darling children. That's the major blessing. Next, dear Annette you've had the great consolation even in this reversal of knowing that you behaved with dignity and poise which was noticed and remarked on and of receiving so many evidences of devotion from your own circle and from the public of De Berri[?]. That my dear child counts as real happiness and possessing such treasure in this world we are not likely to value unduly such material things as fate can take from us. However, I do regret the loss of your lovely chain of amethysts and the ring but I must admit my dear that I can't imagine why those items weren't kept with your other gems. If you had worn them the day before then I suppose it is admissible but here a maid puts such jewellery in a basket and locks it away until the next day or else puts it directly in its accustomed place. In case of an accident then, the whole safe or table is carried out. But according to what you tell me, the pearls were also left out and were only saved because your waiting woman climbed the ladder, wrapped them in a piece of flannel and threw them out the window. This I can also understand because apparently you wear them every day but they should nonetheless be put away properly. I hope that you will recover most of your gems and maybe once they are cleaned and polished they will be almost as good as new. The coloured stones are lost, I am sure. But in time the amethysts might be restored. Unfortunately not many have been found lately in Siberia but occasionally some are brought in. Since the silver from your dressing table was found you could have another made up but tell me, what happened to the one of vermaille. I am distressed that my letters to you are gone, dear Annette. Many memories went with them but so long as I am alive my dear child, you can leave such things in my hands and when I die you will have your letters back and so you'll have a record. I am delighted that the King offered his help so promptly, but I don't understand why William had to buy a house for you to live in. I had thought that the state would provide for him as heir to the throne. I don't think my dear that you will have any great difficulty in re-establishing your library. Since you didn't have any precious manuscripts you'll find everything can be replaced. You should send to Paris where they often sell libraries, both as individual books and *en masse*. As for the Russian books, send me the list of the lost ones. Villanof has already taken care of the things you asked him to look after and will report to you next Wednesday. You are a noble and powerful lady, my dear child. I hope too that the revenue from your dowry and the allowance from your inheritance which I sent have helped. The devotion of your household is most gratifying and your Russian valet seems an excellent example. Your priest also is a most distinguished man. The little Brussels waiting woman seems to have behaved very well. Were you pleased with the Chernichef family? Sybourg certainly proved herself in running to help you without any thought of her own belongings. That's just like her and will make her even more dear to you.

### Tuesday 18 January

I have undertaken, my dear child, to send you by the first ship a copy of my portrait as well as that of the late Emperor and those of your younger brothers. I have also looked after your Russian books and will send everything by sea. The courier who's bringing things for the chapel, the priests vestments and the furnishings which I am sending will be too burdened already to carry much more but he will bring you a great store of tea and thank you for letting me know that you needed it. It makes me very happy, satisfies my maternal heart to be able to do things for you. I am glad to see that you are going out visiting a bit. It's a duty of your position so that I believe that isolation is as misplaced as too great a love of distraction. Moderation in all things. I see by the public press that the people were delighted to see you attending the theatre. Your poise and noble bearing enhances the esteem they have for you. That's worth having. Good night my dear child.

## *Wednesday 19 January*

My dear child, I am sending you as you asked an account of your capital assets. There's another more detailed list which the treasurer couldn't give me immediately as he had other work to do. But it will reach you on Saturday. You realize my dear that you are a rich and powerful lady. The 20,000 roubles which I gave you the year I was in Moscow are still in the Bank of Moscow but if you agree I will have them sent here so that it is all together. In that case also you will have to send back the bank notes from January the 2nd, each for 10,000 1818 roubles. I have a proposition for you my dear which I believe will be to your advantage. Thank God the value of silver is going down and paper money is increasing in value. It used to be 1 to 4. At the moment it is 1 to 3 roubles and 11 or 12 kopecs and will certainly keep falling. Therefore it would pay you to change the assets which you have in silver and gold to paper money while excluding 50,000 roubles in silver of dowry which you haven't touched. If this proposition appeals to you, you will have to give Monsieur de Villanof written authorization to act for you very gradually, asking him to convert your gold and silver assets and suggesting that he continue that course with your future resources. That should increase your holdings by some 300,000 roubles as well as the interest on that, another 15,000. But this can only be done carefully. Gold has lost a little less than silver. You would also have to send me your cheques from the Lombards which are payable in gold and silver. You will see that the enclosed list of your assets only goes up to January the 1st, 1821. The 20,000 roubles which you have been sent this year aren't included. The 10,000 roubles from January the 7th have already been added to your account however and the other 10,000 will be on February the 3rd. So you are richer by that amount. You will also notice as I asked Villanof to indicate on the list, that since these accounts are up to January the 1st, 1821, the annual interest on your dowdry, just over 22,000 is calculated in with your dowry. But since then, of course that interest and more, to a total of 29,000 roubles has been sent to you. Therefore the actual balance is some 22,000 roubles short of what is listed. And with the dowry as it stands, totals 500,000 roubles in silver. If you wish therefore you can dispose of 102,413 roubles and silver as well as 21,295 roubles in gold. This has been a very dry business letter my dear child but I hope it's useful to you and for that reason I've been happy to undertake the task and know that you will appreciate it as its meant. Adieu my dear. Best wishes to your William and your charming children. Here's the inventory of your jewellery. There may be a few things missing but nothing of significance. Michael and the Countess send their love.

## Friday 21 January

I am so sorry my dear that you lost the superb pearl earrings which were part of your trousseau and also those which William gave you. They could only be replaced by great good luck for they were of superb quality, and I come back to my theme. Why was not all your jewellery in the same safe place? Did you forget a chest in the house? I spoke to Duval this morning to seek whether he had any beautiful teardrop pearls. He said he did not as they were very difficult to find but that he would look out for some. I'll ask at another jeweller who is very much the rage here and will report back to you. As they have already found some of the gems my dear, we can hope that eventually most will be recovered. Perhaps some of them will be damaged but the majority should be all right, not of course the coloured stones or the pearls. Here's the list of Russian works which I am sending by the first ship so, my dear, you will re-establish your national library. Tell me if you want any works by other authors, dear Annette.

## Saturday 22 January

I already sent you a letter in the mail, my dear and am just writing these few words to tell you of my visit to the community to hear the children perform a chorus from Haydn's *Creation*. They also sang some duets by that same wonderful composer. It will soon be the end of term, the closing ceremonies will be on February 20th, the last day of the carnival. Carnival is a very lively time here. There will be many private balls, Michael has been invited to several.

## Sunday 23 January

I am glad to have the opportunity of sending my gifts by this courier so that you will have them a bit earlier. The 10,000 roubles and the topaz bracelets are for your birthday. The topaz cross is for your name day in February. It's fashioned in a totally new style. I do hope you like it my darling for it's quite unique. I thought it was so lovely that I wanted you, my Annette, to be the first to have one. I am enclosing the usual 10,000 roubles for your name day and I am also sending some of the very best tea and will send more by our regular courier.

## Tuesday 25 January

Duval will gladly carry out your wishes as quickly as possible, my dear, but he thinks you should know that those stones which need to be repolished, some of the diamonds and rubies, should be done in Holland. He has to send them there in any case because here it's not done that well. So my dear you should entrust those stones which need repolishing to a reputable jeweller in Holland and then send them here to be set according to your wishes. I am sure I will soon be able to send you the rings which were rescued from the ruins. As for the teardrop pearls, there are not any available here at the moment but Duval is looking out for some. The Empress went to visit the community this evening and appeared pleased with the music, the deportment and the dancing of the children.

## Wednesday 26 January

I forgot to tell you yesterday that Duval said you should keep the lovely coloured stones of the late Princess of Orange as they are very rare and truly beautiful. He means the pale rubies from Brazil which are not often that perfect. He estimates the large stone to be worth 800 roubles and the earrings at 500 roubles.

## Monday 7 February

Dearest Annette. A courier arrived from our dear Emperor who is very well. I am going to copy out the part of his letter which refers to you and you can just imagine how pleased I am. 'You will see from one of my preceding letters that I already knew of the fire at Brussels. We must of course be very grateful that there were no worse consequences of the accident. As well however we must think how we can make up some of the losses suffered by my sister, especially of her trousseau. Dear Mama, may I rely on you to direct and guide Monsieur Gourief in this task? You have always been very generous to all my sisters in making up their trousseau. It seems to me that it would be only right to replace anything lost in the fire.' You see that Alexander hasn't changed so let me tell you that having notified Gourief of the Emperor's wishes, I also said that I knew you wanted the beautiful pearl earrings replaced as soon as possible and that you had asked me to find two beautiful teardrop pearls. I told him that I had already been to Duval who said that none were available that he knew of but that he would look for them. I requested that he give it his best attention. He promised me that indeed he would and would wait my further instructions as far as replacing the rest. So, now, I am asking you my dear to send me a complete list of what you would like replaced. I assure you my dear the list you send will be attended to and dear Alexander's wishes respected, but you must feel free to ask for what you need. I was very pleased with the examinations which went extremely well.

## Thursday 10 February

I must tell you my dear child that I went to the Grand Theatre yesterday with Paul. We saw a beautiful ballet. The room is beautiful but it seems to me a bit small for the public of Petersburg. This evening I hosted charming entertainment at my place. Your brothers and Paul are invited out every evening to balls in the town which is very amusing for Paul. Good night my dear, it's late. I love you very deeply.

## Monday 14 February

The public examinations for the community ended today. The audience was enormous so that the room was crowded. The public was quite satisfied and they told me that the children conducted themselves very well. The music was successful. We have some delightful voices. The dancing went very well and our overall appearance was everything we could hope for. My sons and Paul attended the examination and came back quite enchanted. It's certainly the most interesting graduating class that we've ever had as far as character, knowledge, talent and style. Michael can't get over it. The ministers from abroad were also in the audience. These dear children leave on Sunday. My blessings and best wishes go with them. I will miss them.

## *Tuesday 8 March*

. . . I begin by saying that your letter which arrived yesterday evening delighted me. I see that the state has decided to build a palace for William. I hope that you will let me know where it will be located. It seems to me that the King has behaved very well in this matter and I thank God for it. Nothing can be more pleasant than to see normal family relations as nature intended them expressed in an obliging and affectionate way. Everything is going very smoothly here thank heavens. You will be glad to know how well thought of Nick has become. People were extremely pleased with him on his last trip. Michael is still the same fine young man, passionately interested in the military. May God grant him a happy marriage in the near future.

## *Wednesday 9 March*

Greetings, my dearest. The courier's leaving this evening and the roads are quite dreadful. I am sending this small gift to William for his recent birthday. I remembered how much he likes malachite and have sent him a clock and a press (pressoir) which has a Russian peasant on it. I am sure that William will like being reminded of the national costume of our people. I am sending you, my dear child, a collection of engravings which has come out here recently. It has portraits of the family from Czar Alexis Michaelovich on. You will find it interesting as many of the portraits and engravings are extremely well done. I am also sending you some pages of the map of Russia and Poland which have just come out. For your two oldest darlings there are swords like the one I gave our youngster here. The jewellers where Duval sent the diamonds which needed polishing is *Charles and Sons of Amsterdam.*

## *20 March*

We heard from our dear Emperor yesterday but he did not say anything about coming home yet which is disappointing. The revolution in Piedmont is extremely ugly. It's unfortunate to see the evil and the misfortune spreading. The Empress already came to visit me yesterday so you know that she is well.

## *Tuesday 19 April*

I have just said good-bye to Paul and I am really upset by it. I am very sorry to see him go. May God keep him. He is a wonderful young man and I love him dearly.

## *29 April*

Dear Annette. I have been looking after your interests and I've been busy with details for Count Gourief for Duval with all the things you've entrusted to me. I find that your list is very moderate and certainly there's nothing to omit from it. Indeed your great delicacy has caused you to leave out many objects which I am sure you'd love to have. Duval is starting to set the circlet [guirlande] and the rings. The diamonds haven't lost any of their sparkle. Duval is also looking after your special instructions for the bandeau and the necklace of teardrop pearls.

## *Monday 9 May*

I had a great reversal today, dear Annette. A terrible fire burned 108 houses to ashes at Federovski and another burned down part of one of my best villages here. I am especially sorry about Federovski whose inhabitants are wonderful people. I am going to Pavlovsk tomorrow to bring what help I can to the unfortunate villagers.

## *10 May*

I am just back from my trip to Pavlovsk, dear child. I saw the poor people and spoke to them to console them and to tell them what we can do to help. They are sad but resigned and left me with their hearts reassured. There's considerable loss. Even the church is damaged. The priest's house burned down. But as of tomorrow we will start the work of outlining the village and rebuilding. God will bless us!

## *15 May*

I'm taking the opportunity of this courier from Nik to write both of you. I don't know when the letter will reach you as I've asked Nicholas not to send it on by mail but to see that it is delivered to you personally. He said it would be impossible for William to visit us because the King was indisposed. Believe me, my dear girl, if the King's legs are [—] it's almost a guarantee of health and long life. Besides, the King's colour is good and, in any case, if William feels he can't come to see us now, just how does he think he can manage it when he is King? So, I'll have to give up the hope of ever seeing you again because I will never agree to separating you from your husband for six months nor to you making the trip alone. My dear Annette, it wouldn't be right and I don't want it on my conscience. Let God be our judge, dear, which of us is honouring His word. William solemnly promised me, Anna, to bring you back to me. I'm still waiting and he's the only one who can give me the joy of seeing you for a visit. But I don't want it at the cost of allowing something I think is wrong, this separating man and wife. My dearest child, I'd never do that.

Since heaven has granted you three sons and the first is almost five years old, perhaps he could come with you, although we must recognize that your children belong to the state, therefore we can't act as ordinary citizens but must accept the established customs of the state. I don't see any danger. In case you do make the voyage, I don't see any problem in entrusting the young children to your mother-in-law. It's only natural, as who else could be solicitous, so why would there be any hesitation or doubt. I'm sure the Emperor said the same thing when he saw William but after all it's up to William when he will bring you and once that is decided, everything else will fall into place.

I'm exceedingly distressed to see how the King is treating you both. It's very sad. He's only poisoning his own life but then that's nothing new in my opinion. Unfortunately, he's never been well disposed to you but what really upsets me is that I understand from your letter that the relationship with the Queen is no longer as strong and friendly as it was. This is a great sorrow to me because I was so happy in thinking that you had a caring friend in your mother-in-law. How did the coolness set in? For heaven's sake, my dear child, do even the impossible to revive the warmth between you; devote all your energy to it. She's always been so good and loving with William that you must re-establish those dear bonds. The Queen is so good that, in spite of her innate reserve, she is a truly loving person and always seemed to be really fond of you.

My dear Annette, I've written this like we were talking face to face.

## Pavlovsk
### *25 May*

Dear Annette:

Yesterday I had the pleasure of welcoming Alexander at Gatchina and found him well and very glad to see us all again. You can imagine how happy I am! I can't even talk about it. We talked until almost 6:00 p.m. and then he left for Czarskoeselo and an hour later I left to come here. Today I saw our dear Emperor again. It doesn't seem possible but he's more wonderful than ever. He's one of those people who get better and better. We talked a lot about William. He was so glad to see him again.

Good night, my dear child, I forgot to tell you that the Emperor thought I looked very well. So, you see, there are no more signs of my sickness.

## Pavlovsk
### *Tuesday 31 May*

With the next courier, I'll send your necklace of pearls and a small bundle of rubies which has been reset and is very pretty.

### *Thursday 9 June*

The dear Countess was very happy to have her son, Christopher, and his two sons arrive for a visit. The oldest has a very distinguished bearing. The younger, Constantine is quite the young Englishman, and pronounces his French as if he'd been born in England. The dear lady is extremely happy to have her children with her. The count hasn't changed at all. He's just as he was when I saw him in Brussels.

## Pavlovsk
### *15 June*

Since there's a courier for Nik, my dear, I'll send your necklace of pearls repaired, some beautiful pearl earrings, a gift from the Emperor to replace the ones you lost, your bandeau of rubies and 54 rings which have been reset. I hope you will be pleased with this consignment. The first courier will bring your circlet of rubies. Please send a receipt for the earrings, the bandeau and the rings in this package and for everything you've already received so that I can give them to Count Gourief. I'm very sorry that I already sent off the letter covering the last few days but I admit that I forgot that this courier would be leaving soon and all this morning and early afternoon I had business to attend to. Then I had the pleasure of a visit from the Emperor and Empress which lasted until 6:00.

I suppose that you must be at Spa already and that you've seen Nik. That must have been a happy reunion. And I suppose you've met his charming wife, who I'm sure you will love dearly. Our dear Emperor is in good health and, thank God, he looks wonderful. I'm very well, too, dear Annette, and try to get as much exercise as possible. The weather, though, is still cold. We've had only one beautiful day and today again it is really cold. I hope it is not like this at Spa or the bathing will be spoiled.

## Pavlovsk
### *9 July*

Dearest Annette:

You'll have heard before us that Napoleon died on May 5th by the new reckoning. We heard that he slipped peacefully away after an illness of 40 days. I trust he repented of his sins, seeking the Divine mercy. What effect did the news of his death have in your country, my dear? I must admit that I don't think it makes much difference. His position made it impossible for him to participate in world affairs. However, perhaps the end of his career will stifle future factions from forming.

### *Sunday 7 August*

What do you think of the death of the Queen of England, if in fact it is confirmed? She should have died before her trial. It would have been better. Nonetheless, her death will benefit England because the hotbed of intrigue has lost its centre and will be extinguished.

### *Monday 22 August*

I am appalled at the scandal which erupted at the burial of the Queen of England. That unfortunate woman was the centre of trouble during her life and still is in death. It's terrible that blood was shed because of her. The much vaunted English freedom has many disadvantages and what can we possibly say when we find out that the Lord Mayor himself is among the leaders of the trouble.

## *Sunday 4 September*

The Emperor came to the Institute after Mass and went over it thoroughly. He seemed to be very pleased with the building and with the way the property is being kept. He was also pleased with the children and was astonished with their progress in singing which is going extremely well.

## *Thursday 8 September*

Many thanks for your letter, my dear child. Today's gazettes mention an anonymous letter which William was supposed to have received from a French crook which threatened his life if he didn't send 20,000 francs. If I'm not mistaken, the gazette said that the man had been arrested at Rambouillet. Apparently William had notified the police in Paris of the letter. Is that true?

I've had good news from my children in Warsaw. They are going to leave on September 1. My nephew, Eugene, has arrived and I'm looking forward to seeing him tomorrow. I was very interested in everything you told me about Mademoiselle M—. They say she's a wonderful actress and it's annoying that she hasn't come here. We have an actress who they say is like her who is very pleasing.

Good night, dear Annette. My best to William and to your little battalion.

## *Saturday 10 September*

Nicholas and Alexandrine have come home, dear child, in good health. Both much thinner. They are very pleased with their travels, especially happy with their stay at Spa, and really touched by the friendship you and William showed them. They told me all about your children whom they think are charming. The youngest one must be very good looking. To all intents and purposes, my whole day has been spent walking on air. I'm eager to see and talk to my dear family and I'm so pleased to have them back.

### Tuesday 20 September

You'll be thinking today of your respected and worthy father. You'll keep him in your intentions. You'll offer prayers for him just as I have done. I'm going back to the church again. I wish it so much that you could be with me, my dear Annette, but at least I know that we have the same sentiments and are both asking the Supreme Being, in His infinite mercy, to grant everlasting peace to our dear departed.

### Thursday 22 September

We've had good news from our dear Emperor who was well satisfied with the condition of his troops and the manoeuvres which were just completed. They say that the general effect was superb. At the end of the manoeuvres, the officers begged the Emperor to honour them by accepting their invitation to dinner. The officers' table was for 700 people and the whole company of the Guards, more than 30,000 men, lined tables which had been prepared for them. The whole of the army drank the Emperor's health with shouts of joy. The Emperor drank to the Guards who always and everywhere have distinguished themselves with honour. Such a toast so true and yet so flattering was enthusiastically received.

### Gatchina
### 28 September

Michael arrived here last night after my letter had already left. I was happy to see him so well with a prosperous appearance. There's no lingering trace of sickness and he assures me he feels marvellous. He's gained back his weight, his *joie de vivre* and is finally our old Michael again. Thank God. I will admit that I was most anxious about him all this last winter. The dear Emperor dined with me very well and in excellent humour. His presence always spreads satisfaction and serenity. Our weather continues to be reasonable and I make the most of it when I can.

### 5 October

I always await your letters eagerly, dear Annette, and this time I will say with considerable curiosity as well about the details of the King of England's visit.

They say he has always been very fond of William so he will have been glad to see your husband but I'm curious to know if he wasn't a little embarrassed about meeting you. The gazettes announced his arrival in Calais. He seems to have been very happy with the reception he received.

Our weather continues pleasant. I take advantage of it to go out with my dear Michael who, thank God, is again in good health, body and soul.

## *Friday 7 October*

Duval, on Mr Gourief's instructions, gave me this safe which contains your circlet of rubies which can be worn as a tiara, your beautiful diamond fringe, the centrepieces of your rope of diamonds, a number of rings, two clasps which you wanted altered, one with the sapphire you got Duval to buy, and the beautiful drop shaped topaz which William gave you. I hope everything will arrive in good condition. In three or four weeks the rest will be ready. Duval told me that the cabinet had supplied him with some very beautiful amethysts. I'll be anxious to know that the courier has arrived safely. He'll go to Stuttgart first with a letter to the King and then to you, whether at Brussels or at The Hague.

Thank you, dear Anne, for your last letter which came in the mail last night. But you haven't satisfied my curiosity about the King of England in the least. *Except for his upset stomach*, you tell me nothing special about him. His way of behaving generally and towards you and William in particular. Please send me all those details by courier so that you can comment freely. I see that they are *putting on the dog* [*fait grand frou frou*] for him in Brussels. The gazettes are comparing the splendour of the entertainment they gave him with that given to the Emperor Francis in 1794 and for Napoleon and Marie Louise when Napoleon came to Brussels the last time *as a conqueror*. I must say that I was astonished by that comment. How did he behave to the King and Queen? Especially, how did he behave towards William? What are you and dear William doing? With Alexandrine, we often talk about you in your situation. Try to be patient and resigned, my dear children. Your happiness comes from yourself, in your union, in your children and in your good conscience knowing that you have nothing to reproach yourselves with. I always say, as does the Emperor, if you have behaved rightly then there's no need to concern yourself further. I believe you are about to move back to The Hague. I wish you had taken this opportunity to come and see us, my dear children. How happy we would have been.

As for the children, I still believe, and the Emperor is of my opinion, that you wouldn't run any risk in trusting them to your mother-in-law. I admit that I'm afraid that the longer you delay your visit, the harder it's going to be to get away. I often talk to Alexandrine about your children. She is a great advocate of your oldest son. It seems to me, judging by the portrait or rather the drawing you made for Prince Volkonski that he still has his sweet face. Why didn't you also draw young Frederick Henry who they say is so handsome? Tell me, my dear, did you receive the portraits I sent you and the books for your library? I sent it a long time ago.

Thank God you must already know the really good news that we have. It seems, and may heaven be blessed, the great cloud which was darkening our horizon has cleared a little and that we've avoided war again. Certainly our dear Emperor deserves the blessings of his country and the rest of the world for he needed greatness of soul and magnanimity to meet all that jealousy from Paris with calm, patience and moderation. His name will be blessed for centuries to come.

## Gatchina
### *19 October*

Dearest Annette:
May heaven bless and protect you, my child, so that this fourth pregnancy will have as happy a delivery as the other three. I thank God that you are well and feeling no inconvenience but I know, too, my Annette, that now that you have experience and know what to expect, you will bear with the necessary courage and resignation all the trials which are almost an indispensable part of pregnancy. I'm sure that you'll take reasonable care of yourself without giving way to those petty fears which are so harmful. I hope that the trip will not bother you but I will be delighted to know when you are settled. I'm also sure, my dear Annette, that you'll have the good sense to enjoy being at The Hague as much as at Brussels and that you'll ensure that you'll be as loved by the people.

### *Sunday 30 October*

My dear child:
I must thank you both for the geraniums, the bulbs and the rose bushes. Everything arrived in good condition except for the geraniums which

suffered in transit. One plant is dead but I think the others can be saved. I was extremely pleased to see them and send you my thanks for this most precious gift. My gardener and orchardist are thrilled with them. How I wish I could offer you the flowers and look after your bouquet as you did mine in Brussels during that visit which has given me such happy memories.

### Wednesday 2 November

I received your last letter, dear child, and will tell you what I've done on your behalf. In future I will endorse your bills of payment for your secretary. Gourief will then be told that you wish to receive the September–December portion of your pension from cabinet early in January. I've also asked the founding home when they are to receive the interest on your dowry that is invested with the Lombards. The term is up on February 9th when we receive our payments in silver and, according to the regulations, interest can only be paid when and as it is due. However, the Lombards can advance part of the interest and can send you as usual by Count Gourief, namely 15,000 roubles in silver coin in January and the other 10,000 on February 9th which is the date fixed for paying out. I'm very glad to have been able to arrange this for you.

### Thursday 3 November

I visited my establishments for the Daughters of Soldiers and the Institute for the Deaf and Dumb. There I learned of a great loss. The death of our most accomplished student. Perhaps you'll remember her. She'd already become a mistress and teacher at the Institute. She was special for the goodness of her character and her great intelligence. She died like an angel in perfect acceptance. We lost her after a haemorrhage caused by the shock due to the death of her brother-in-law. Her sister had asked her to come without saying why and when she arrived and went into the room, there was her sister's husband laid out on the table. She was devastated and as it was a delicate time of the month for her, she lost her blood in such a rush that a few days later she was dead. It's an irreparable loss to the Institute and old Gouffret is greatly distressed.

### *Thursday 10 November*

We've had frightful weather, my dear, but it hasn't prevented me from going to the community. I've dined in their company and this afternoon I received an invitation from the gentlemen of the council of the community to spend an evening there to celebrate the 25th Anniversary of my patronage. The children will have a little ball and supper. There will be a few [adults]. The children are thrilled to be preparing a surprise for me. They are very sweet, very lovable.

### *Sunday 13 November*

Yesterday evening the council invited me to the large hall where the children gave me a very touching party. There were songs and dances; the room was decorated in excellent taste by the council which wanted to celebrate the 25 years that I've cared for the community. It was so touching that tears sprang to my eyes. The gentlemen of the council have given such proof of attachment to me that I couldn't help but be affected. The children acquitted themselves with perfect grace. They were angels.

### *Tuesday 22 November*

I'm relieved to see, my dear, by the letter received from you today that the courier arrived and that you were pleased by the diamond jewellery which was prepared and sent to you. Today I saw the diamond bandeau and the reset amethyst chain which is superb. Count Nesselrode told me that he will soon have a safe courier to The Hague who will bring you those things which will certainly please you. Truly the chain is magnificent and the amethysts are the most lovely colour. It's very difficult to find any like them any more.

### *Saturday 26 November*

My dear child:
I have your letter in which you mention your preparations to celebrate your Queen's anniversary. I can well believe that you gathered all your energy for this day which should be important to you and, please God, everything will go off very well. You tell me, dear child, that your

thickening waist reveals your pregnancy but as you are in the fourth month, you must not lace yourself any tighter than is necessary to support your back for to restrict yourself now may be dangerous for the baby and the mother and certainly makes labour more difficult. *As you are a mature woman*, expecting for the fourth time, you will know to avoid anything harmful. I'm waiting for news of Marie in Memel and my heart is pounding with joy. How happy I'll be to hold her in my arms and how happy I would be if I could embrace you, too.

## *Wednesday 14 December*

Marie and her husband have just left to dine at Czarskoeselo. I stayed with her until she actually got in the carriage. I'm so greedy for every moment I can have with her. Unfortunately, time is limited. Thank you, dear Annette, for your last letter and thank God for your good health. If you have a daughter, my dear, this thought delights me for it will increase your joy and certainly your good husband will welcome her happily.

Goodbye, dear Annette, I'll send you a fond embrace, all my blessings and my dear, dear love.

## *Wednesday 21 December*

I see that dear William's birthday was celebrated appropriately and fondly by Their Majesties and I'm entirely delighted. I'd really like, dear Annette, to have a few more details in your letters and have you discuss things a little with me. You tell me so little about your children, not giving me any details on their sweet ways, their games, what they're doing, their mannerisms, and I'm interested in everything about the little darlings. All these personal details about you, your husband, your children can't compromise you and I'd like to hear them.

## *Thursday 22 December*

Count Nesselrode told me that Gourief received the news that the ship which was carrying your mirrors and your porcelain to you had suffered some damage and had to put into Norway. But fortunately all your things were saved so that the only inconvenience is that they will be late arriving.

## *Tuesday 27 December*

Count Nesselrode had already told me that you had looked after our wrecked ship in helping the crew. I was delighted to hear it but I was already sure you would have as I know your good heart and your love for your Motherland. You have seen in my preceding letters that the ship which was carrying your things also suffered some spoilage but that nothing was lost. It put into a port in Norway. This autumn has been disastrous to sailors. I don't ever remember seeing hurricanes so frequent.

# 1822

## 1 January

Dear Annette:

I will renew my blessing and best wishes for the New Year. May God make it a happy one for you and your husband and children and may your happiness grow with the birth of your fourth child. I expect it will be an easy delivery judging on your good health. I send my love to dear William and your children. We've just come back from a masquerade. I've never seen so many masks. Supper was served at the theatre as usual with beautiful crystal decorations. The foreigners were most impressed.

## Sunday 8 January

Your birthday, dear Annette, was celebrated very happily. After Mass many people came to congratulate me and I told them that I would mention their names to you. The family had dinner together at home and we drank to your health. Our dear Emperor gave the toast. At night there was a magnificent ball in our beautiful hall where we had had dinner and which had been redecorated in white marble for the visit of the King of Prussia. It is superb. The Emperor thought that the ball would be perfect there so that's where we danced last night.

To general satisfaction, supper was served in the Guards' Room. The gowns were magnificent and the ball truly spectacular. I forgot to tell you that Monsier de Voorstoon[?] came to congratulate me before dinner. I asked him to convey my regards to the King and Queen. I hope he won't forget.

## Monday 16 January

I just received your last letter telling me how happy you were to see the snow and hear it crunch under your feet. I can understand what a pleasure it gives you as it reminds you of our dear Russia. On the other hand I must admit at this white shroud depresses me especially when it last seven or eight months.

### Tuesday 17 January

I had the pleasure of visiting Michael's Institute of Artillery which is in the old building where the widows and the deaf and dumb used to be across the river. I was very happy to see it. The Institute is most promising and it would be impossible to take better care of children. Everything is in perfect order and the children seem very happy. My dear Michael is dedicated to this Institute and it is a noble and beautiful cause.

### Friday 20 January

I attended an examination in history, geography, languages, chemistry and natural history at the St Catherine's Institute and was very pleased with it. Our methodology is much improved and does more to develop my pupil's ability. Then I went to inspect my school for the Daughters of Soldiers which interests me very much and is doing very well. They are charming children.

### Friday 27 January

Congratulations, dear child, on our dearest Michael's anniversary and we will be celebrating it tomorrow. Make God keep him and grant him the happiness he deserves. You will be happy to hear that today his future is being decided on. The courier from Stuttgart has brought confirmation of his coming marriage to Princess Charlotte and everyone is delighted. They say she's exceptional and will make Michael happy. Everyone says she's an angel, both in her face and in her temperament. All this makes Michael very happy.

Good night, dear Annette.

### Wednesday 1 February

How pleased I am to hear of your happiness in the love and tenderness that you receive from the family of your dear husband. The letter which you wrote to me gave me great pleasure. I'm not sure, but I find in his letters a feeling of friendship and trust which goes right to my heart. He expresses his proofs of friendship in a way that makes them even more precious. I wish I could see him giving lessons to his beautiful children. How pleased you must have been to see the little angels preparing a surprise of reading to you for your birthday.

I understand how happy you must be. Who gives geography lessons to the boys? Is that William's responsibility or yours, dear child?

## *Sunday 5 February*

You asked for your will, dear child, and it's enclosed here. I am very happy to be able to send it back to you. It was too painful for me to keep it as I should die in the natural course of things a long time before you. The same courier is bringing the rest of the diamonds. You will find the amethyst chain beautiful and also the diamond headband. Duval has followed your instructions for the pearl earrings and hopes that you will be satisfied. Finally, dear Annette, I'm sending you your present for both your birthday and your name day. It is this topaz comb that can be worn either in one or three parts. I'm giving you two for your birthday and the third one, the middle piece, for your name day. The jeweller will tell Chernichef how to separate them. I hope, dear child, that you will be pleased and will wear them sometimes. Here, also, are two 10,000 rouble bank notes for your birthday. Marie is sending you a bracelet.

## *Monday 6 February*

I'm sending with this the small layette articles that you asked for, dear child, and the gold-threaded cushions. I did not include the mattress because it would have taken too much space and you can find that easily in The Hague. I'm sending you a small silver-threaded bonnet for the christening. If you have a girl, the bow should be in front but for a boy, it should be worn on the side. I've added the small chemise and a dozen others with small bonnets and some clothing like a little girl wears here. You see that I'm expecting a little girl that I would love dearly and who would make you very happy. Dear William, I am sure, would receive her with love since his battalion of boys allows the coming of a pretty young lady. I hope it will all arrive in good condition.

Thank you, dear child, for your letter of today. All the details on your children are very interesting to me. Little William's progress is truly remarkable but perhaps he shouldn't study quite so hard so soon. Too much dedication may even be detrimental to his physical development. I understand, too, how his progress, due to the love and care of his father, must interest you. What do his grandfather and grandmother say about it? They must be so pleased with the children. I thank God for the good will and the perfect relationship between the King and the Queen and your dear children. Their Majesties have asked Monsieur de — to convey their gratitude for the part that we played in this better understanding. This happy state of affairs will stop many an intrigue and will strengthen the government. At the same time it will assure William a happy and easier future for he will find in the obedience, the tenderness and the trust of his sons the reward of his filial love for his father. The lesson of his good example will be profitable to all. Harmony in the family is of the outmost importance to ensure peace in the state. I would even say that it's more important in our time than it was in the past. Certainly it's only by maintaining an irreproachable virtue and the strictest attention to his duties that the Prince will have the moral authority to hold his loyal subjects to control the malcontents.

### Tuesday 7 February

This courier will also be the bearer of the jewellery you asked for. Count Gourief sent me this piece containing the last of the jewellery which you asked for after the fire. I will take advantage of this safe opportunity to tell you something in confidence, dear Annette. Now that Michael's future is decided on and that Constantine's example won't influence him any more, in other words, now that the order and custom established by ruling houses has been re-established, I have given in to the wishes of the dear Emperor and your brothers and forgiven Constantine for his marriage and granted him my pardon as of December 12. I have, for the first time, named his wife in my letters and recognized her as my daughter-in-law. I am very sure that she will behave appropriately as Princess of Lowicz. Constantine was very happy and so was his wife who behaves perfectly and never presumes. Your husband, who knows her, must mention her favourably as have your brothers and Alexandrine. I've never spoken of her or mentioned her name in public so all is as it should be. But Constantine is very happy for being forgiven.

### Wednesday 8 February

You will have heard with pleasure, dear child, the future of our dear Michael is decided and the Princess must be charming and the difficult circumstances she's been through have given her a depth of soul and made her very self-possessed. I can't give you the date of the wedding yet. It isn't really decided on and the young lady, though she is in her 16th year, isn't out yet. She seems very well brought up and everything looks as if Michael will be happy, as he deserves to be.

## *Saturday 18 February*

I am sending you the letter of exchange for the interest on your capital, 63,808 roubles and 35 salls[?]. The paper which I've attached will explain clearly why the total interest on your capital for 1821 is all here. I expect as the sum is very large it will be enough to discharge your debts. If not, you could withdraw, as I indicated to you in my last letter, some more money from the interest so far accumulated this year, all or part of the interest on your gold and silver deposits. That way, dear child, you'll keep to the rule strictly adhered to by your young brothers and your sisters of not using the interest on the capital I gave you which still only comes to the sum of 18,000 roubles from this year included in the capital but which is only credited to your account from January 1st of this year. Your reply will enlighten me as to your wishes and needs.

I've just returned from my school for the Daughters of Soldiers. It's doing wonderfully well. What pleasure to see the progress of the children. They already work so well but they're given — from private firms to do. They're beginning to embroider very nicely. They make shoes which are very successful as they have an excellent embroiderer from Paris to teach them. Everything is doing very well on all counts.

I'm glad to see that you're pleased with your organizations as well.

## *Saturday 4 March*

We've just learned that a volcano has formed on the Aleutian Islands. There's a disturbance of the interior of the earth and the sea because the change of seasons is too abrupt.

## *Friday 10 March*

I just discovered this morning on opening my safe that I've committed an unpardonable error. I sent you two Lombard notes for 10,000 roubles on your birthday and your name day but instead of sending you yours I sent Michael's which I gave him for his birthday on January 5th and this morning when I went to take out Michael's note from my safe so that I could give it to him when I saw him today, I found yours from January 7th. I'm including it with this letter and beg you to send me back Michael's. As far as that's concerned, I expect you've already done that having discovered my error before I knew of it myself. I apologize most humbly. At least there's no harm done other than to have brought Michael on a futile trip but your Mama is such a *scatterbrain* due to her great age.

### *Tuesday 21 March*

This evening we went to the community with Marie, her husband and my nieces. The children sang, played the clavichord and danced. They performed like little angels. Talent is greatly developed here. You'd be pleased to see the Institutes, my dear, and we try to show ourselves off to advantage.

### Gatchina
### *Thursday 6 April*

I set off yesterday, my dear Annette, before I wrote to you. It was a beautiful day. It would have been even for a day in July. It was 18 degrees in the shade. I stopped at Czarskoeselo where I left Marie for a few hours while I went on to Pavlovsk. Everything is springing up. I gathered wild flowers. Nature's ahead of herself by some four weeks. I visited my orangery which delighted me. I saw some superb flowers. When I returned to Czarskoeselo, Marie and the Prince joined me and I came here as the evening was divine. Marie was so happy to be here and this morning and afternoon we were outside all the time and very gay. How could not we be with weather such as this. Tomorrow, to my great regret, we return to town visiting Pavlovsk on the way and dining at Czarskoeselo.

### *Friday 14 April*

I was very sorry to hear of the death of your cantor and will see his good wife as soon as she arrives. I'll also see to it right away that the two children are placed as boarders at your expense and will see if the younger girl is the right age and meets the other admission requirements to be admitted herself two years hence. The new admissions won't be for two years now as a new group entered last year. As for the wife, my dear, since her husband wasn't an officer or rather didn't have a commission, she could enter a home for widows and become one of that order but I'll see if I can find her a job as I do feel a bit responsible for her. I'll let you know what I'm able to do when the children arrive.

## Sunday 23 April

Yesterday evening we went with Marie to visit the building of the new community. It is quite handsome, very large, containing many interesting objects from Peter the Great's time. It has his personal ship models and a collection of signed letters as well as a wonderful library and the beginning of a museum which we owe to our sailors. You'll be happy to see these things.

## Pavlovsk
### 13 May

As the Queen is absent for a few days I trust that you will show your gratitude to her by waiting until she gets back before you allow your little girl to see the light of day. I admit to you, dear Annette, that I believe you will give us a fourth boy and in truth that's something to be proud of. Today is Paul's wedding day and God grant him all the happiness that I wish for him.

## Gatchina
### 22 May

My courier to the Emperor has left and hope from there he will go to The Hague to give you my congratulations on your happy delivery. What a blessing! I can't resist writing to you the second letter of the day. How I wish I could see you now in your bed with four sons around you. Your mother is radiant. I was frightened to hear that the Queen had a fall. I haven't said anything to her because I know that people don't like these misadventures to be talked about but I thank God that there was no damage done.

Good night my dear mother of four little boys.

### Sunday 28 May

I saw your minister today, dear Annette. To entertain him this evening I played whist because he doesn't know Boston. He seemed to enjoy himself. We were very pleased with him. He speaks well; he is forthright and intelligent and his regard for both of you gives him a real claim to our indulgence. He seemed to like it here.

### Tuesday 6 June

The date today reminds us all, dear Annette, of the Battle of Waterloo and I thank heaven that our good William was spared. I received your letter written two weeks after your delivery and I rejoice in your good health and the regaining of your strength. I don't think you've ever recovered so quickly. I see that you're very happy with the care that our good Harry and the new obstetrician are giving you. You are fortunate to have people you can have confidence in and that in itself contributes to the recovery. The weather here isn't as good as that your're enjoying.

### Pavlovsk
### 13 June

Here I am, home again. This morning I went to the community. Then I dined at Camionostrof and after dinner the Emperor took me to Gelaghin Island and I saw the apartments which he is having done for me which are delightful. They unite elegance and beauty. Everything is finished beautifully and all the furniture and crystal was made here. It is delightful. Especially the office which is painted imitation marble. It's a real ideal of elegance and beauty. This arrangement will mean that when I'm in the city I will have the pleasure of being near to the Emperor. The garden is divine in a beautiful English style. This kind attention of the Emperor's is very, very precious to me as are all evidences of his love.

### Monday 19 June

Finally, dear Annette, I've received some letters from you and can be reassured. The gazette said the new baby wasn't well but as you haven't said anything about it I trust that it wasn't true especially since you tell me about his baptism which had to be held immediately in Amsterdam. This time, my dear, it surely won't be you who carries the child to the altar. Since it's only three weeks after the birth you won't want to expose yourself to that fatigue. It wouldn't be wise. I'm sure that the setting of the date, the 6th/18th of June, will make William very happy and such a kind attention from the King must be very precious to you, my dear child.

### Monday 17 July

Our dear Emperor came to bid us farewell as he's leaving tomorrow for [Czarskeselo] so that he'll arrive at Peterhof on the 20th. The Guards are gathering there. Most of them have already arrived. There will be a military review of the troops near Strelna. The date isn't set yet but the Emperor must leave on August 4th for the Congress of Verona. You can imagine how much this absence distresses me. The Emperor, too, feels it deeply as it's hard for him to leave his country and his family but he constantly sacrifices himself for the general good. He deserves to be blessed by the whole world.

### Peterhof
### 20 July

What do you and William say about everything that has been happening in Spain? I'm devastated. We'll see a replay of the atrocities of the French Revolution. What's your opinion of this Monsieur de Alava? What ignoble conduct but also what a reflection can be made on the King's behaviour. Truly, it's a most unhappy episode.

### Friday 28 July

The great military parade was just after 9:00 this morning, dear Annette, on a large plain near Strelna. I'm sure that your military heart would have been stirred, dear child. It was beautifully done. The Guards have never looked better. The weather co-operated as we had only a few drops of rain. There was a crowd of spectators. Monsieur de Croquembourg was dazzled with the spectacle; the Regiment of the Hussards especially impressed him. He said he'd never seen anything to match it.

### Gelaghin Island
### *31 July*

I wrote you yesterday, dear Annette, by Monsier de V— who hadn't yet left. I'm delighted to be in this enchanting place which is both elegant and magnificent. The house is perfectly executed, the garden is delightful and very English. The growth there is extraordinary. There are a great number of oak trees two or three centuries old. Our dear Emperor, out of the goodness of his heart, arranged everything and his thoughtfulness anticipated all my wishes, all my tastes. In fact, I've never been so perfectly suited. The lawns, the vistas are very, very beautiful and the lovely neva enhances the countryside.

### *Monday 7 August*

My God, my dearest Annette, how I wish I could be with you to help care for your dear invalid. I'd be able to see how he is with my own eyes. I still hope, dear child, that the shunt will avert damage. I remember how the famous F— told me how he had cured a child with that condition. This person is even still living. Let us hope for divine protection and trust ourselves to it. I know how much you and William are suffering. You did very well, Annette, to pray. Strength, courage and trust in the true and I'm very glad that you are preparing to make your devotions. Heaven will bless you. The harm is very serious but his case isn't hopeless. God grant that by Thursday I receive good news, dear Annette. I hold you next to my heart and share all your suffering, my dear. May heaven help you.

### Pavlovsk
### *10 August*

Michael's letter is coming by Warsaw so it will take a few more days to arrive but Marie tells me that you told her that Charlotte has got much prettier and mature and that she is charming. This praise from him pleases me enormously. I'm impatient to get his letter to see what he has to tell me.

### Pavlovsk
### *13 August*

I received letters from our dear Emperor written on August 9th. He's travelling comfortably and is very well. Michael also writes me that he's very happy with his betrothed who he finds quite grown up, prettier, charming, graceful, making an excellent impression. He seems very pleased and it seems that he has finally fallen in love. God grant that it lasts for his happiness. Everybody says the Princess is an angel. Michael is very shy and reserved with the Princess in public but when he finds himself with her and he's at his ease, that's to say with people he knows well, he's all heart and soul. I thank God and I'm sure he'll be a good husband.

## Pavlovsk
### *16 August*

Lately, de Croquembourg has lost his high spirits. He fell in love with young Princess Xilnof, a maid of honour, a very agreeable girl, sweet and well brought up. She went to the Institute of St Catherine. He told the Countess, asking her to speak for him to the girl but the young lady refused his suit. She doesn't ever wish to leave her country and her parents. That refusal has made him very unhappy. He became hypochondriac and got thin and he was so moved that he wept bitterly. Fortunately, the stay at Peterhof and Gelaghin where these young ladies wait upon us alternately meant that he doesn't have to see her every day and it seems that he's tried very hard to get hold of himself. What proves that his love was true is that he never spoke to her more than the others. His conversation with all the young ladies was quite ordinary, but he was struck by her kindness and sweetness. I was really sorry, for one could see that he was unhappy. The Emperor wishes him well, as we all do. I'm telling you about all this because you might learn of it from others and I know that the Countess has written to you about it. She would have preferred that as soon as the young lady said that she didn't want to marry him, he would have immediately stopped loving her. The Countess was angry at his tears, but the Countess expects a perfection from us which is more than men are capable of. We must demand it of women, but men don't follow the same strict rules. And Croquembourg, truly in love with Xilnof and refused, was profoundly moved, even to tears, though he didn't allow himself a word of particular conversation with her. I think he's to be pitied. I hope that when he is back home he will forget about her and be as light hearted as he used to be, I really hope so. I've given to Croquembourg the chest with sable furs which the Emperor asked the cabinet to arrange for as he learned from me that you wanted one to give the Queen as a present. He immediately ordered that it be seen to. It's very kind and gracious of him. It's very beautiful and this gift from you to the Queen will give great pleasure. Here also are two more chests with lace which I am asking you to send to Madame Kirt[?] because . . . so that they'll be sure to reach her, and here too, my dear, is my gift for the birth of your baby. I hope that you like it and hope that you'll often wear it. It's the latest style. May this trifle please you. Here's a ring for Harry which I beg you to give him in recognition of the care he's taken of you. Thank God, dear child, that everything is going smoothly in your country and certainly one can say Russia is the most fortunate country in Europe. May God return the Emperor to us. Then my fondest wishes will be fulfilled. Croquembourg will tell you how good the Emperor is. Nik is very well. He is putting on a bit of weight which suits him well. He's working a lot and the Emperor is pleased with him. I'm happy to know that Michael is happy with his betrothed and really in love. I predict his happiness because he is good at caring. By all reports the young lady must be charming. Your happy marriage, my dear, is the joy of my life. May God preserve it and prolong it til the last moment of the King's reign. Then William will thank heaven for his happiness. You've spent a very pleasant winter in Brussels, dear child, and certainly everybody will be pleased to see you back. How is the house progressing? I've received your will, my dear, but I tell you it still bothers me to have it. I should die before you, my dear child, and a long, long time before at that. So, wouldn't you do better to keep it at home.

## Gelaghin Island
### *18 August*

Dear, Dear Annette:

My poor child. How sorry I am for you. How keenly I feel everything you're going through with this poor, little being who we'd hoped to save. This morning I received your letter of the 2nd to the 5th this month and reading it tore my heart for I have no more hope. However, my dear, what is impossible for man to accomplish is possible for God. Let us put ourselves in his hands, my darling, and you will find strength, courage and acceptance in your religious belief and in William's dear example. Tears are only natural, my dear child, but you must not allow yourself to collapse. Your child, if he is taken, will be an angel in heaven who will pray for you. His soul is pure and will go back to God if indeed he does not live. Well, my dear, I know how you wish to see this dear soul as much as possible now and how you cling to the life that this beloved child has left, but you must still take care of yourself for the sake of William, the other children, your mother, all of us. I've experienced this misfortune many times and still feel its pain. I can identify so much with what you must be feeling, my darling, but in the name of heaven don't let yourself collapse and control your nerves. As Mons de Croquembourg is coming to take leave of Alexandrine today, I have asked him to come here as well so I can tell him of your cruel fears and give him a few words in a letter for you. How I wish I could come to you, to William, to be together, to share our pain and take comfort in each other. Dearest Annette, I think of you constantly and I can see your pain. I've anguished at the thought of what Monday's mail may bring you. How glad I am that the Queen visited you. Her presence was a blessing for you and her tenderness will have replaced mine. Tell poor Harry how sorry I am for him. He's so sincerely attached to you and your children that he must feel dreadful. What is Sibourg doing? She must also be suffering cruelly. Oh dearest Annette how cruel it is to be separated during these times. Farewell my darling, my dear child. God grant that the little one may still receive my blessing. May heaven help him.

## Pavlovsk
### *17 September*

I amused myself this afternoon and evening by looking at my folders of sketches and drawings and it's obvious that I have no little drawing of yours, dear Annette, done when you were a child. Please send me one from that time. I'm sure you've kept some. I have some of your brothers and sisters done at that age and I want to have some of yours as well. Your beautiful drawings are still my great pleasure and the most beautiful ornament in my room. I'm making myself a small album. It would be very kind of you to send me a little drawing for it. As to size, I'd like it to be a bit smaller than your usual letters but I beg you, dear Annette, not to do it in black crayon as it erases so quickly. It needs to be a red marker which keeps much better. You see, my dear, that I'm counting on your compliance.

I'll say good night now.

### Sunday 15 October

You tell me, dear child, that you're taking yourself in hand to receive presentations to see people and that you go out to theatrical presentations. I will grieve that you owe the first duties to the people of Brussels but I don't see why you torture yourself by going out to entertainments while your heart is breaking. That's not necessary. William will decide if I'm right, of course, but I'm writing what I think.

### 28 October

You realize, dear child, that if God has tried you with this misfortune, He has also heaped blessings on you. You are a happy wife and a happy mother of three superb sons. Heaven has spared them and time will soften the bitterness of your sorrow without ever making you forget your child. But you'll think of him as a soul in heaven who will be for you, William and the children a guardian angel. The Empress asked me to give you her kindest regards. She didn't want to write you during these first days of your loss but she intends to soon. Here's a letter from Nicholas, from Alexandrine and the Countess.

### Saturday 11 November

I hope that you have taken up your pencils and your brushes again. You must develop your talent. I hope that you stay in Brussels, that is itself pleasant and favoured with a good climate. It will provide you with distractions which will help you to recover. How happy I am that the family has been so supportive. That state of affairs must offer some consolation. God grant that it may last as knowing dear William's principles I'm sure it will. I'm sorry that Madame de Fagel is not with you. Is Mademoiselle Oultremont her equal in your friendship and love? Talk to me about Brussels. It all interests me.

I've got only good news from here of Nicholas, his wife, his delightful children; of Michael, who's in good spirits and happy. The portrait of his betrothed is lovely and he says, as do those who went with him, that she's even better than it portrays. They say that she has an angelic character. Michael thinks so, and if he's not in love with her, at least he's perfectly cognizant of her virtues.

# Chère Annette

### Sunday 26 November

I'm sure you have been thinking of the beautiful anniversary of today, dear child, and maybe you will have remembered the lovely ball I gave in 1814 on this date which Tolstoi arranged and which was so successful. This time, in the absence of the Emperor, we spent the day very quietly. I received good news from our dear Emperor which makes me very happy in that he tells me he's going to keep exactly to his promise and will be back during the first days of the coming year.

### Wednesday 29 November

I saw in the gazette that a Dutch theatrical production was going to establish itself in Brussels. Is that so? They say that Talma will be there this winter. I rejoice with you because I know you enjoy seeing him in different roles. Do you often visit the theatre and is the quality as good as ever? Ours continues to decline. I'm especially sorry to see that our Russian actors aren't being trained so that the young people destined to replace our old actors are very mediocre.

### Saturday 9 December

You are letting yourself go on the slope of discouragement, dear Annette, and you undermine your health and thereby your happiness and that of William and the children because you really become ill. For heaven's sake, accept what has happened and become your usual self, dear child. Concentrate on all the things which heaven has blessed you with. Once before and still on the same subject, I remember saying that as heaven has given you such a beautiful bouquet of sons, you could well give yourself a rest and then come to visit us. I think I remember that Croquembourg said with his usual frankness that he would say as much to the Prince. The feeling I find throughout all of your letters causes me inexpressible sorrow and pains my heart. In heaven's name, don't give in to it. You damage your nerves and you'll fall into a depression worse than any sickness. You must guard against this state by moral action and remedies.

## St Petersburg
### 10 December

It was after I lost my poor Aileen[?] and nine days after her birth I was desolate as it was also the first great sorrow I had ever had and as weak as I was I thought I would die. I remember that two weeks after the death of the poor baby, the late Empress gave a party in the Moorish Tauresque Palace during the carnival. As I was still lying in I wasn't there. The Grand Duke was good enough to stay with me. My brothers and sisters were at the party of the Empress who was offended that the Grand Duke wasn't there. I'm telling you this story, my dear, because I remember that the thought of that celebration hurt me deeply and people were astonished and disapproving of me for it. I think that especially at Brussels, my dear, you must be careful to continue to win hearts by your sweet way of receiving people and being with them. You're doing William a great service and you both know people like to be entertained by you.

### *Monday 11 December*

It's seven years since I met William and I daily thank God for giving him to me as a son. The wife of the Prince of Orange has duties to the public and can't follow her own inclinations to withdraw too much from the world without hurting herself and especially her husband. He must win the hearts of the people and to do that must make himself known. You see, dear Annette, that Maman is writing to you as she speaks and will always speak to you. If William thinks it's necessary to give a ball I'm sure he's doing it for good reasons. He must please the public and court them and insult them at his peril. It would be working against him. So be of good heart and courage, dear.

# *1823*

## *Wednesday 3 January*

The cold has become dreadful. Beside the river it is 18 below. It's intense so that we feel it even in our rooms. At least it's sunny so we can't really complain. The last letter I received from the Emperor tells me that he's met Charlotte and the good impression she's made on him. He thinks that she is very suitable in every way and has a charming face. As well and more importantly, everybody agrees that she has a sweet temperament. Therefore, I can hope that Michael will be happy, even as happy as Nicholas is. His wife is delightful and lives for him, anticipating his every wish, all his thoughts; doing everything she can to please him. May God keep her safe. Certainly I couldn't hope for a better daughter-in-law. She is perfect in all respects, therefore she's not only cherished by the family but is also very well regarded by the people who, as you know very well, are not easy to please. But she has won everybody. The dear Countess sends her love.

## *23 January*

Dear Annette:

I have just received your letter dated the 3 to 6 of January by the old calendar and answering mine of the 17th to the 20th of December. I am very sorry to see that you have misunderstood the loving concern of a mother; that you think I'm reproaching you though I was only preoccupied with worry and fears for your health and the wish to relieve your misery with my advice. Again, I solemnly promise you that your letters are the only source of my anxiety. I've kept them all to re-read with you and you'll have to admit that on all accounts they would have to disturb me. I had the dear Countess read them all as well as my answers. I've even kept copies of those in which I have spoken unreservedly in response to your letters. I am always scrupulously careful so that even if my letters should be intercepted the most disinterested reader could only find friendship, tenderness, concern and my loving care for you, my dear child, as well as for William and your children. How could my words reproach you when no thought of it is in my heart and you don't deserve it. In my letters I see *you are suffering*. Can I then remain untouched? You are the one, dear child, who in your letters has told me so many things which I had no idea of and I repeat that I have no other source of information. This is what I predict, dearest child. Your goodness, your gentleness, your sweetness will always win hearts and then you'll be content, my Annette. If I do speak frankly, dear child, in the letters sent in the mail it would be because it would be impossible not to answer your own written with so many details and the omission might even be misinterpreted. All my letters show my great love for you, unreserved trust between you and William will smooth everything over because you have a common goal, that of your mutual happiness. How very happy I will be, dearest Annette, to see you both here this fall. Tell me often about your plans. It will help me anticipate the happiness in store for me.

## Friday 26 January

I see, my dear Annette, that you have nursed our dear William during his illness, that he is now better and that you have been to see the Queen together. You found a perfect balance, my dear, in fulfilling William's reasonable request that you attend the Queen at the ball for the nobility since she had to be there, leaving right after she did to attend to your duties as nurse to William. That was very well done and I rejoiced at your account. The gift from the King and Queen must be superb. You tell me that you have been given so many beautiful things. Itemize them for me. At least what William gave you. I'm interested and I would like to know.

## Thursday 15 February

I was delighted to see Constantine today who paid me a surprise visit. Only the Emperor was in on the secret. Constantine is very well and in good spirits. Good night, dear child, I'm collapsing with fatigue.

## 17 February

I'm just back from the examination, my dear child, which went extraordinarily well. It was religion, Russian literature and translation. It was only an individual and preparatory examination. Next week there will be the examination before the council and myself. I'm not easy about your plans for the celebration. I strongly advise you to do as I do. I wear a piece of waxed taffeta lined with linen over my left side where I've had a pain for 25 years. When the pain is too strong I rub the linen with opadeldon[?] and that relieves me. The Empress is almost well. I'm sending you the bank notes for the 25,000 roubles of interest on your dowry. Please send me a receipt.

## Saturday 24 February

Dear child, I must leave for the last examination at the Institute. It's a display of talents. It won't be as long as the others but I must be there soon. The public examination is going to be Monday and Tuesday. Then the council will complete the evaluations from Friday to Monday. If I am pleased with the music I will invite the Emperor and the Empress to hear it on Saturday and Sunday, the 4/16 of March. The children leave. I'm always sorry to see them go to their family.

## Wednesday 28 February

I want Alexander to be happy. I need to have his approval. Perhaps you know already that Paul's wife has given birth to a son so here I am, by the grace of God, a great-grandmother.

## 20 March

I rejoice in the spring sunshine. It beautifies everything, especially when it's shining on something as lovely as the park in Brussels. I see that you're happy with these little evening parties which sound so agreeable. You tell me the Queen was a guest at your entertainment and that she laughed wholeheartedly which always does a person good. I'm also happy to see that you're thinking about your trip. That you are making your plans. You tell me, dear child, that you want to send your effects by sea. Wouldn't it be better to follow Marie's example who sent all her things and those of her ladies by cart a week or two ahead of her? It's more dependable and your clothes wouldn't be so likely to be damaged or spoiled which happens sometimes on a sea voyage. Also, you can estimate the dates of departure and arrival of a cart while you don't really know when it comes by sea.

### *Saturday 31 March*

I'm leaving, my dear, for the school for the Daughters of Soldiers. It's the anniversary of its founding and I'm going to distribute the prizes for good conduct and application. The school is doing very well. The children's achievement is astonishing considering how recently the school was established. We're going to establish another one for the Daughters of Soldiers in other regiments. That's an example of how the Emperor continues to extend his good works.

### *Tuesday 3 April*

May the holy duty that you've just accomplished strengthen your courage, your submission to divine will, your acceptance of your suffering which is part of this world and the total trust in divine mercy and goodness. I can imagine, dear child, how touched you must have been with William's goodness in accompanying you in your devotions, even to wearing a Russian uniform. That's just like him and I am delighted for you, my dear, who can appreciate such an attention.

### *Cold Saturday 21 April*

I have so much to do. I just received your letter this minute, dear Annette, and I'm sorry that William can't come with you but as he must be absent so long this fall, it is natural that he should wish to stay near the children and, of course, he will come to visit you. We won't go to Moscow, dear child. It's the price we pay.

### *Tuesday 15 May*

What date has been chosen to go to the waters and baths at Ems. All the letters from Berlin talk of Marianne who they say is very interesting. Her appearance must have developed and become very agreeable. Her manners are pleasing and generally people praise her. They also say she's very good. I dined at the Hermitage and we went to the Gelaghin for tea where I had the pleasure of seeing the Emperor and the Empress.

## Pavlovsk
### *Thursday 18 May*

The great military parade took place, dear child, and it was magnificent. Truly we're approaching perfection. The Emperor was very pleased and your brothers were happy to have Alexander's approval. The parade lasted four hours and as it was sunny and windy, I was so sleepy that I could hardy keep my eyes open.

### *Thursday 24 May*

It was a delightful morning after the rain and I took advantage of it to go for a walk. Pavlovsk is very beautiful. I haven't ever seen the countryside more beautiful or brilliant. I went to your pavilion which will soon be ornamented with lilacs in bloom. This evening I heard a nightingale. There are several in the garden. Nature is at her most beautiful and it looks as though we'll have a good harvest. God grant it.

### *Monday 4 June*

I've just received your letter, my dear, telling me of your departure the next day and that of the ship carrying your things. The Emperor has given me the authority to write to the Minister of Finance so that your cases won't be opened. They will be delivered to the Winter Palace. I will notify Monsieur de Naryshkin, the Court Marshall. Now, I am really beginning to believe that you're actually coming, dear child, and I'm so happy. May you have good weather and good roads. I regret that the Emperor won't be here when you arrive. He's leaving August 16th/28th to make a tour of 4,000 or 5,000 versts to visit the provinces and the armies so that he won't be back until the end of October or the beginning of November. In the meantime, your Maman will receive you and William as best she can.

### *Tuesday 12 June*

I'm very pleased to see that Marie has won over your entourage but that's what I would have expected as everyone says she's delightful. I learned today that you will be seeing Catherine's poor little orphans. They're charming children and I never think of them without heartache.

### *Sunday 1 July*

I've had a tiring day, dear child, which followed a tiring evening before. We celebrated Alexandrine's birthday with a tableau — and a little comedy put on by the ladies and gentlemen of the court. It was all very successful and pleased Alexandrine. Today we had a Mass, an enormous dinner and a ball but your brothers had to leave us after the dinner to return to camp and we didn't really have the pleasure of the Emperor's company as he stayed at Czarskoeselo with a lot to do and needed also to rest.

### *Sunday 8 July*

We had a charming children's ball this evening. It was quite delightful and the young people were very sweet and very well behaved. Nicholas' children were good enough to eat. Even Olga was with them. She's beautiful enough to make hearts break. Your brothers came back from the military colonies delighted with what they saw, blessing the Emperor for this monument of glory which will contribute so much to the happiness of our nation. May God keep this Emperor who does so many good deeds.

### Pavlovsk
### *14 July*

I reproach myself for having neglected letting you know, my dear, that the ship with your belongings arrived almost two weeks ago and that your things were delivered to your English lady. I saw your valet who came here to see me. It's all in preparation for your arrival so I can tell you, my dear, that I was happy to see him. I beg you, my dear Annette, to send me an exact list of the number of your carriages and of your entourage, servants included. Next, send me your itinerary and specify on it the day you will arrive at Memel. You'll be happy to arrive there and you'll find quite a grand society there as Charlotte will be with us by that time.

### Gelaghin Island
### *8 August*

We had the most beautiful parade, dear Annette, in the most beautiful weather imaginable. The Emperor was very pleased, and well satisfied with the work of his two brothers which made them, in turn, very happy. It lasted four and a half hours, almost five hours, as more than 40,000 men were in arms. The evening was also very beautiful and we went out. Gelaghin Island is charming and very animated. Every evening there's a crowd of people there. As the weather was beautiful, we had a lovely outing on the water coming back by the most gorgeous moonlight. The island was bustling with all the people who'd come to listen to the music. Then we went out again in a carriage as the evening was so beautiful that we didn't want to stay home. The moonlight is magic at Gelaghin.

## *Wednesday 15 August*

Today our dear Emperor bids us farewell. It's a sad day for us. He's coming to dine here, then he'll stay visiting me awhile and then we'll take leave of each other. May heaven heap blessings on him and watch over him wherever he goes. There are more than 5,000 versts to go. It's a frightening thought but at least he'll be in our country. Michael leaves us on the 17th to see his brother Constantine and to go from there to the border to meet Charlotte. Nicholas leaves us on the 20th to go to the camp at B—.

## *Friday 24 August*

Dear Annette:
Your letter of the 4th/16th of August has arrived and I won't try to hide from you, dear child, that I felt such an emotion, I'll even say considerable pain, in seeing the hope of seeing you destroyed for this year. But, my child, I collected myself immediately and won't allow myself to be distressed because it's contrary to my duty. Your condition, if you are pregnant, is another blessing for you, another proof that fate is good to you. May God's will be done. Certainly you're both behaving as duty and prudence demands in not exposing you to a trip in that state, if it is indeed confirmed. Tell yourself, dear Annette, to take courage and to put all worry out of your mind. Keep your gaiety.

## *Monday 27 August*

I'm delighted with their [the children's] intelligence, their frankness, their confidence in William and you. It is evidence of your mutual happiness. Why do you say that poor little Henry, who everybody says is so nice, has a different character than his brothers? Is he less light-hearted; less lively? Often that's a factor of his body type. The fact that a child develops more slowly only means that he'll develop better. If you are pregnant, I hope you have a little girl this time without really setting my heart on it, as William has predicted you'll have six sons.

### Monday 3 September

The Minister of Finance answered that as soon as the ship arrives your things will be sent to the court's courier who is also being notified but I'm hoping that it hasn't arrived at Cronstad yet. I regret that Monsier de Fagel's presence deprives you of the pleasure of seeing his gracious wife. She's in a sad and upsetting situation. I'm just as curious as you, my dear, what's going on during the conclaves. Intrigues will be rife as always. I confess, though, to my way of thinking, it's not a position to envy.

### Wednesday 5 September

My dear, there's a great *commotion* today here for the birthday of the Empress. There'll be an entertainment. They're putting on the *Pie Voleuse* by Rossini. The music must be very beautiful. I hope it will be well researched and performed but that's what our actors are generally lacking.

### Tuesday 18 September

We have weather fit for the gods, dear Annette, but I wasn't able to take advantage of it as I went over my whole castle to see the arrangements made for the arrival of my guests. I'm trying to renovate Gatchina as much as possible. It was really neglected during T—'s administration. I've had letters from Marie before and after Charlotte's stay. She seems very pleased with her and thinks that she'll make Michael happy. May God bless her! The poor child has had so little happiness in her life to the present that we can hope divine providence will make it up to her.

### Monday 24 September

Michael sent me a courier to announce his arrival at Polange[?]. His reunion with the Princess at Memel after doing 760 versts in two days and 17 hours and the arrival of Charlotte at Polange. Everybody is enchanted by her and finds her angelic without being truly beautiful but the expression of her face is preferable to actual beauty. She must have unbelievable poise for her age. She spoke Russian to the officers who were presented to her. Michael must be behaving very well towards her taking care of her and paying her all due attention. As well, he's in excellent spirits. He found the Princess had really changed and grown up.

### Sunday 30 September

Our dear Princess Charlotte joined us this afternoon. I saw her yesterday. She wasn't expecting me and the interview was very touching and pleased me. She is charming though definitely not beautiful. I would even say that she is attractive in the sweetness of her expression, her charming manner, her wit, her character, her tact, her education. At her presentation she won general approval for she managed to say something pleasant and appropriate to everyone. Not at all common. We are all enchanted. May God keep her like this. I can't say much more about her, dear Annette, it's impossible to be much better at 16, more mature or more reasonable and she is pretty even though she is not beautiful. Her complexion is very like Marie's. Many people find a resemblance between them. She has gained our approval and truly she is charming. She's reasonable, witty, tactful, poised and has pretty skills. She is delightful.

### Sunday 7 October

We had many people here and there was a ball. Charlotte dances very prettily with becoming reserve. She's very graceful in everything she does and her tact never fails her. The poor Empress is very worried about the health of her sister, Amelia. She seems to be toxaemic. It's frightful and distresses me a great deal because I really love Amelia.

### Tuesday 16 October

Dear Alexandrine is well. Her children are delightful and the little boy is so beautiful and at the same time has an angelic character. Little Marie is grace personified while Oline is the most beautiful child I've seen in my life. She's also very gay and promises a great vivacity of character. Charlotte is a little indisposed with stomach cramps and being a little delayed but it's not serious. She's already better today. I went out in the carriage with Charlotte and Michael. We went to feed the deer. You know this outing, my dear, we've often done it together.

### Tuesday 6 November

I went to Czarskoeselo to visit the Emperor and the Empress. I dined with her as the Emperor was receiving Prince William of Prussia and all those gentlemen. I stayed with the Empress and we dined with Antoinette. Since the Minister of Prussia and his wife are staying with me I had to chair the evening and be charming so I'll admit that I'm all tired out. I see you're displeased with Harry. However, my dear, I must say that I think he's a good doctor. I know that sometimes opium is given to a pregnant woman to calm her cramps and a diet of vegetables and fish which he ordered didn't surprise me. Here everybody is preaching a frugal diet, eating as little as possible.

### Monday 26 November

William is here, dear Annette, since 7:00 this evening. I am so perfectly happy. He's looking very well, just the same as ever. William is very glad to find everything, so to speak, in its appointed place in my rooms. He feels he's never left. When he went to visit Charlotte, who is living in your rooms, he had the feeling that you were just coming to meet him so strongly that he thinks Charlotte is like you in general size.

### 27 November

Truly, you couldn't have pleased me more; they'll always be with me. I'm delighted to see you taking your old pleasure in your art. You must not neglect such a distinguished talent. I haven't yet had much chance to talk to William. A thousand thanks for the lovely bracelet which I have on my arm. It made me extremely happy. I showed William the first one you sent me with the hair of your oldest son. Also, many thanks for the two caps and charming shawl which you so kindly sent me. Everything is very lovely and you are determined to make your old Maman beautiful. I'm very grateful, my dear. Thank God I've got only good news to send you about dear William, dear Annette. He's well. He went to the parade of Semanofski's regiment which was superb, to Michael's great satisfaction. Michael's engagement is set for the 6th of December, the Feast of St Nicholas. Charlotte will make her profession of faith on the 5th. I'm sure she'll do well.

## Monday 3 December

Just imagine the goodness of dear William who had the delicacy to pay his respects to the tomb of our dear Emperor. I didn't know of it until after his return. His sensitivity and refinement in doing this touched me deeply. Charlotte has begun her devotions. She studied her religion well and thinks over everything she does. She's an accomplished person who I hope and trust will make Michael happy.

I'm just back from the confirmation of our dear Charlotte who has taken the name of Princess Helene. She did her part with a devotion and an emotion which were really admirable. You would have been her sponsor if you hadn't been pregnant, dear Annette, but because of your condition there's a convention against it which had to be respected. So, Marie was the sponsor.

## Thursday 6 December

They exchanged their promises this morning, dear Annette. Helene was very sweet and Michael behaved perfectly. I am very pleased and happy. Thank heaven! Helene had a blue velvet outfit all embroidered in silver rosebuds and leaves, beautifully done. The skirt was full and the border of the skirt and the train had a magnificent embroidered design with roses. She had an emerald diadem which was closed by the comb. A superb emerald set like Alexandrine's with a clasp for the collar and earrings and a beautiful chain of diamonds with Michael's portrait. In the evening there was a state dinner in the marble hall in the Emperor's wing and later a state ball in the Hall of St George. You'd have thought that Helene had grown up as one of the family. She's astonishing. At the church William said to me, 'What memories this ceremony brings back to me,' and his eyes were full of tears.

## Monday 17 December

Today I took William to the community with me as well as Helene. They both seemed very pleased with the respect shown by these good children in the beautiful hall. The beginners' class performed a bit of music and then all the classes danced. It was a truly charming sight and our children acquitted themselves very well.

## Thursday 20 December

Our dear William will tell you himself what a reception the people gave him at the public entertainment we went to yesterday. All of society was there. The theatre was very well lighted. They put on *The Cossacks* and the *Ballet of Flora* and *The Zephyr*. People were glad to see Helene who they say resembles me so that she looks like one of the family. I find that she occasionally really reminds me of Marie. This evening I had a French entertainment put on for William. They did *Valerie*. Our leading actress performs the role very well and William seemed pleased. There were a lot of people there, too, and William thought the supper room very well done.

## Monday 24 December

I've asked William to take you this talisman bracelet set with turquoises and a turquoise pin for your palatine brooch. Think of me, dear Annette, when you wear them, knowing what pleasure I have in giving them to you. I've sent sabres and swords and uniforms for your boys as I think, at their age, they'll enjoy them.

## Tuesday 25 December

The church ceremony lasted a long time today. You know that the Te Deum for the deliverance of Russia was included. We were standing for more than two hours. Helene was as pale as a ghost. Sweat covered her face and she couldn't see straight but endured and didn't leave the church. This young lady certainly has command of herself. Generally she's a most estimable person and I'm sure William will praise her to you. God grant that Michael appreciates her as she deserves. At present he isn't as impressed as I could wish even though he gives full credit to her merits and worthy qualities. I believe it is due to the awkwardness of being betrothed. The celebration went off as is customary. After Mass there was a formal dinner at my palace then I went to give commemorative gifts to my grandchildren which delighted them and made them happy.

## Friday 28 December

This day has painful memories, dear child, which I'm sure preoccupied you, too. Poor dear Catherine, I always feel her loss and ache for her. Perhaps you already know that this is also the date of Helene's birthday. From now on we'll celebrate it on January 1st but for this time we gave her our gifts on the day and when I went to see her after church, I changed from my black dress. William will tell you all our news and give you details about Nik, Alexandrine and their children. May God keep them all. I've never seen a happier marriage or charming children. Nik is the most loving father and Alexandrine a perfect mother.

## Monday 31 December

I thank heaven that you are well and am very glad to note the kind attention of the King in coming to congratulate you on the Emperor's birthday. I'm sending you your will, dear child, with William as you asked. I've resealed it for you because you sent it to me opened. Congratulations on the marriage of your brother-in-law, my dear. They say your future sister-in-law is a fine young person. I hope that she'll be a friend to you and an agreeable companion. It's so pleasant when one has friends in the family. William enjoyed himself here with us and is sorry to leave. He'll give you an account of our assemblies, of my ball and he'll tell you that they're still impressive and the tone is all it should be. He'll tell you all about our pretty little Helene who will certainly please you. He told me so again today. Her character is serious and reflective and she's very sweet. It seems to me that Michael is growing more fond of her and I'm sure that his feelings will continue to deepen. Michael has such a good heart that he can't help but make everyone around him happy, especially, I'm sure, his wife.

Pavlovsk Palace

Emperor Paul

Empress Maria Feodorovna

William, Prince of Orange

Anna Pavlovna

Tsar Alexander I

Tsar Nicholas I

Brussels Palace

# *1824*

### *Wednesday 2 January*

William left at 4:00 this morning. Our leave-taking was painful to both of us, dear Annette, and our parting conversation was about you and the hope I have of seeing you with him sometime here. We talked until the last minute and were somewhat comforted. Our dear William will give you my present, dear child. Accept it with pleasure. I am very glad to be giving it to you. I also enclose your birthday present of a Lombard bank note for 10,000 roubles and also a second one for your name day. William will give you my present for the latter.

### *Friday 11 January*

May God grant you a happy delivery of this pregnancy, my dear. I expect it of His mercy. I'm sure you will give birth to a beautiful child, easily and quickly, and if it is a little lady of Schlangenbad, we will receive her with joy. One of the Emperor's aides-de-camp is travelling to Berlin to carry official congratulations to the Prince Royal for his marriage and I have spent all the afternoon writing letters. I confess that I am tired after these six letters and can hardly see, so please forgive my brevity.

### *3 February*

You'll be happy to hear dear child that the Emperor is in good health, thank God. He still has to stay in his apartment because of his leg which requires some care so Michael's wedding will be celebrated either the 8th or the 10th of this month in a chapel which has been set in the Emperor's reception room so that he can attend Mass. For the rest, the whole ceremony will be as usual. None of us would consider the possibility of a wedding without him, nothing else matters. All the celebrations will be postponed until after Easter when I will be giving a formal dinner and a state ball and then a celebration at the Tauride Palace with fireworks as we had for your wedding. The next day people will come to offer their congratulations to the newlyweds. On the day of the wedding the formal dinner and ball will be in St George's Hall.

## *Friday 15 February*

You'll be happy to hear, dear child, that I had the great pleasure of receiving our dear Emperor. He came to visit after dinner in order to avoid the guards because he was wearing a robe. He came through the waiting rooms and William's room. You will know how happy I was and this will tell you that thank God his leg is healing. William would be so pleased to see the happiness of Michael and Helene. God be blessed! We hope to see them as happy as Nicholas and Alexandrine. It's good to know that the Queen's ball was so successful. It's wonderful to see people enjoying themselves and so unpleasant to read boredom on faces. Nick and Sache are giving a ball tonight. Tell William that all the equipment for his small Hussards is ready. We are wrapping it and I will pay his banker to have it sent to Amsterdam as soon as possible.

## *Saturday 16 February*

Yesterday I forgot to tell you that in the morning I accompanied your sisters-in-law and your brothers to the community to listen to the singing and watch the dancing of the graduates. That class is generally musically talented. We heard a concert for clavichord and voices which was superb for there were twelve of the King's clavichords altogether and the ensemble was truly delightful. Two young ladies at each keyboard. In this way, the concert was executed by 48 hands in striking precision. We have some beautiful voices and all was very creditably carried off.

## *Wednesday 27 February*

We have chosen a lady-in-waiting for Helene. It is the Countess d'Elnet who was married to the lieutenant-general and has been a widow now for many years. We chose her for her excellent reputation. She was presented at court and is an acquaintance of Madame de Solaing. She's very well known by Madame d'Arque. We all liked her very much. She seems to be everything her reputation says. A pleasant woman, sensible, trustworthy and loyal.

### Sunday 16 March

You ask for some details, dear child, about Helene's wedding. She was not wearing the train at her wedding as space was limited but after the ceremony she wore it in the Empress' apartments and walked with it through the halls. The next day she received from the Emperor a set of sapphire jewellery and from Michael a diamond choker like the one you've seen Alexandrine wearing and earrings. From me she received a necklace, brooch and comb in amethysts and diamonds, which with the tiara she received for the engagement, complete the set. For her betrothal, she received from the Emperor a set of emerald jewellery. From Michael, a chain of diamonds with his portrait; and from me the tiara and earrings in the amethysts and diamonds. My tiara has a point in front on the forehead following the latest fashion. For her birthday, she received a beautiful set from the Emperor in rubies with a delightful likeness of the Holy Cecilia. I gave her a brooch, quite beautiful, also with rubies and diamonds. Michael gave her a jewelled fan. I think I've answered all your questions, Annette, and I end by sending my love to you and the children.

### Easter Tuesday 8 April

I just can't imagine you, my dear Annette, round as a ball. You've always been as slim as a nymph. I know you will recover your beautiful figure. The King's generous present of the portraits he was hoping to acquire must have pleased William and you greatly. It's wonderful to see a father that anxious to please his son.

## Pavlovsk
### Friday of Easter week 11 April

Monsieur de Hoof has arrived, dear Annette. I met him this morning between 9:00 and 10:00. I read your note avidly and will keep it with my souvenirs. It made me indescribably happy. We heard the news 36 hours after delivery. William, dear and excellent William, is more than happy. Everything he says proves it. He wrote Alexandrine that he can't stop watching you and the baby. He says, and so does the Queen, you have never been so well. May God be thanked and praised a thousand times. Both Monsieur de Hoof and William mentioned how happy the people are at the birth of a little girl. William says he knows how much the people love you. I stopped at Czarskoeselo and asked the Emperor to give me a courier to send you my congratulations and love as soon as possible. One will be ready tomorrow and meanwhile I told the whole family to get their letters ready. The Countess was so pleased with the news. It's the first time in her life, I think, she's been happy with the birth of a girl. She is absolutely delighted. Who does the little darling look like? I am so touched, dear child, that you named her after me. I hope my name will bring her luck.

## St Petersburg
### *Monday 20 April*

This afternoon I went to Catherinehof to see what has been done. Peter the Great's house has been rebuilt. There are also some slopes for sliding on. In fact, they've also restored a farm. All this fascinates the public and attracts incredible crowds.

## St Petersburg
### *Friday 25 April*

You already wrote to me, dear child, that you were wearing your ordinary corsets the seventeenth day after delivery. Don't you think that's too early? Don't you suffer from it? I've never been able to wear a corset that early or tighten my clothes then. They say it's dangerous to your health.

### *Friday 9 May*

Tonight I read about the christening ceremony. It was a good idea for William to take the dear boys to church for it. They'll never forget it and they will cherish the memory of accompanying their father. I read in the gazette that William rewarded the children beautifully by allowing them to set down the first stone of a new building in The Hague. Children raised with such principles are bound to be successful. I'm happy to see that the little darling has already used the cushion that I sent you.

## Pavlovsk
*15 May*

May God keep you in prosperity and may your children grow daily morally as well as physically. If only I could see them once. It's so cruel to realize that there's no chance of it. I'm often saddened. You must possess a fortune in pearls, dear Annette, and I'm very glad that you do. I'm not afraid of any changes you fear I may notice in your face. I'm not at all afraid. My Annette will always seem the same to me.

### *Tuesday 20 May*

I'm sending you, with the consent of our dear Emperor, the Order of St Catherine for dear little Marie Sophie. You'll put it on her giving her a kiss in my name and my blessings. I cherish your beautiful children. It's so painful to me to think that they don't have any feeling for me because they don't know me. Monsieur de Hoof seems to be a worthy and excellent man, very attached to you, my dear, and to William. Count Gourief has been named to The Hague and to Brussels. His father and mother have both asked me to recommend him to your kind notice. His wife is very self-possessed, very likeable, very pretty. She's a daughter of the Grand — and although she looks a lot like him, she's a striking beauty. At least she was. Since that time, of course, she's been very sick. She's a virtuous woman who will please you so I beg you to be good to her.

### *Sunday 1 June*

Niks arrived during the night in good health but as black as a Negro. He is incredibly tanned but it suits him and gives him the marshall air. We had a lot of people here today and as it is impossible to go out, I had a dance for the young people. Your brothers act like complete invalids and never dance a step anymore. A cotillion at the very most. They waltz briefly when invited by the ladies and even then it has to be Alexandrine or Helene. As for me I played my game of Boston which puts me to sleep.

### *Wednesday 4 June*

I hope that the mail brings me some news of you and that you tell me more about your garden, your plantations, your beautiful orangery. It all interests me a lot and I'm delighted to see my own love of flowers born again in one of my daughters.

## The Winter Palace
### *Wednesday 18 June*

I'll put you in my old rooms in the beautiful apartments which I lived in during the late Emperor's time. I hope you'll like it there where I will be next to you. Send me the exact list of the people who are in your party. It needs to be complete: waiting women, lackeys, everybody included so that I can make sure everybody is provided for.

### *Sunday 22 June*

I saw the Emperor again today to give him my love since he's leaving tomorrow but will be back again on Tuesday. He's going to Grésine[?] and to the military camps as well; and his leg is better. We've had quite a few people here today, but we didn't have a ball since the camp has removed our dancers. The season will have started there, but it's rained a lot. The workers, though, are pleased so I suppose we shouldn't complain. I hope that my roses won't suffer. I hope to have a beautiful crop of them.

### *Monday 7 July*

I have good news of our dear Emperor. His leg is fine. May God keep him. We've been worried about the health of Constantine's wife who has to go to Ems. I hope the waters will do her good. She's a very fine person, and makes Constantine extremely happy. She never presumes. I suppose you'll make her acquaintance and I'm sure you'll like her.

## Peterhof
### *Thursday 24 July*

Our dear Nix and his excellent wife left today. At 3:00 in the afternoon the ship raised anchor and left under full sail. The Emperor and Michael went with them on the ship and stayed until they put the sails up. We accompanied them to Oranienbaum and went with them to the port. That's where we said goodbye.

The children were with us and nothing could have been more touching than to see their farewell to their parents. They dissolved in tears and sobbing, especially Alexander who is extremely sensitive. Their departure was very, very moving.

## *Tuesday 5 August*

I saw one of our diplomats who is being sent to the court at Brussels, my dear Annette. It is Monsieur de Lima, a Portuguese, who was here for 9 years and who earned the esteem of the public by his noble conduct at the time of troubles in his country. During the Revolution he left his service without the means to support himself in order to remain faithful to his King. There's a recommendation for you, dear child, and I thought you'd like to have this information about him.

## Pavlovsk
### *11 August*

Here I am, back home, my dear, with my youngsters. The two little girls came with me. My little Oline asleep in my arms. She is without question the most beautiful child you could hope to see. May God keep and bless her. You would be enchanted by her, dear Annette, as well as by Marie, who is wonderful. William will see how lively Sacha has become. He climbs trees, gets himself out of trouble, I think[?], balances on beams, jumps about and is becoming really agile and active.

## *27 August*

You're leaving today, dear Annette, and must say goodbye to your children. That's the thought that's preoccupying me and distressing me for your sake. It'll be a sad moment. May the joys of motherhood soften the memory of these sorrows.

## Palais Tauresque
### *29 August*

How will you be able to support it? Don't be afraid of being tired, dear Annette, because if it fatigues you to come to my place, I'll come to yours instead. I couldn't really house you and the Prince suitably in your old rooms at Gatchina. You wouldn't have been able to entertain and besides with so many people to accommodate the lower storey is divided into four different apartments. In my own apartments upstairs, I never house anybody but the family. As soon as we're a bit crowded I dine upstairs and receive people upstairs, so you really have just a few steps to go.

### *Sunday 7 September*

It's warm, mild, as agreeable as July. I hope this temperature will last when you have arrived. I'm thinking of you constantly, dear Annette, and am afraid that you'll be overtired. Even though you are coming in very easy stages, the change of routine may tire you. However, once you've arrived, you can rest as much as you need to and I hope you'll soon feel restored.

### Pavlovsk
### *16 September*

You'll be surprised, my dear Annette, to see our dear Michael on the way. He's going to Warsaw and is taking the road you're on in order to greet you. It's a pity that he won't be here when you arrive but I think his presence will be much appreciated by Constantine at this time. He's so worried about his wife's condition and unfortunately I think he has good reason to be.

# *1825*

Pavlovsk

*25 July*

1 0.30 p.m. So I was able to pause and reflect a little and certainly today gives me plenty of subject material. Dearest Annette, how painful it is for me to see you leaving again but you've left in my heart a sweet consolation in the form of your promise that you'll return in two years time.

*Sunday 26 July*

Dear Annette:

How dull everything seems and how I miss having you out in the small garden with William. I know, my dear, that you left a note on the table. Frederick told me but I haven't yet had the heart to go into your room. I'm too upset. Helene came directly here from Peterhof this morning to see me. She's being very, very kind.

*Wednesday 29 July*

I'm sending a linen batiste outfit by the courier who will return with news of you and William and Madame de Wassenaar. It's a present I'm happy to give you. There's also a package which Monsieur Bulganof sent me for you as well as a letter from Mr Weschoski[?] and a rolled packet containing the documents from the exchange which you left here. The translation of the works of M— weren't in your rooms and they told me that your man had found them and took them with him when he followed you. Also, dearest Annette, yesterday evening Marie gave me your will which you want me to keep. Though I'm touched by your confidence, I admit the sight of it distressed me, but as I'm sure to go before you, my friend, allow me to point out that it's only in my keeping for a few years after which it will be sent back to you. So, I'll keep it as you wish, but at least wrap it and seal it with your seal, then you can put it back in the package where I marked the different dates when you've given it to me and that package I will seal and place in my chest with instructions to Villanof that it be given to the Emperor when I die. So, I'm sending you the package in the safekeeping of this courier and if you think it's appropriate he'll bring it back to me. This evening the garrison is alight with fireworks in honour of the grandchildren. It will be opposite the Pavilion of Roses. The Emperor and the Empress are dining with me tonight.

## Friday 7 August

I had the pleasure of seeing the Empeor who told me that the Empress' trip is settled and that the doctors have chosen Taganrog as her winter quarters. Apparently the climate is mild and healthy. You know that the town is beside the Azof Sea. God grant that the doctor's opinion will have the good results they hope for. They say she needs a temperate climate, not too hot, because any overheating of the blood is harmful to her. The Emperor tells me that she's leaving on September 3rd and that he'll go ahead of her on September 1st. He'll be back at the end of the year. What a dreary winter we'll spend, worried as well because of his absence.

## Pavlovsk
### 18 August

All we hear about is departures. It is very sad. The Emperor is leaving on September 1st, the Empress on the 3rd, Nicholas is leaving for his inspections and Michael and Helene are going to see Constantine when he gets back to Warsaw. They are looking forward to the trip and I'm sure it will be good for them and have a lasting effect. The health of the Empress varies. She was very well recently but yesterday and today she's tired. Maybe it's because of the heat which she doesn't tolerate well. This evening we are going to begin reading the famous novel by Walter Scott, *The Lord Lieutenant of Oxeter or The Betrothed*. People speak highly of it.

## Czarskoeselo
### Tuesday 25 August

The weather is beautiful but the Empress is not well, in my opinion. She seems weaker and more overwhelmed with fatigue than usual. Her health is so changeable and that's what's distressing because we don't know why. She looked very ill today. I've rearranged the paintings in your drawing room, my dear, and it's very successful. I've moved the Tiepelo, which was on the right wall, to a place right of where you usually sit. Then the head by Guido has replaced it and the lovely head of Leonardo de Vinci which Michael drew has gone where the head by Guido used to be. It looks good and Michael's drawing is well highlighted. Then I placed a pretty table which I got for my birthday on the side to the right of the writing table so that letters and packages can be placed upon it.

## *Saturday 29 August*

I went to the Botanical Gardens in the droschka. I'm so sorry, my dear, that you didn't see it while you were here. It's one of the most beautiful sights imaginable and I even dare say that it's larger and more spacious and more impressive than what I saw at Weimar. It's a real landmark which the Emperor is constructing and when you return you will be delighted to go for the superb garden which is only two years old and has already survived flooding.

## *Monday 7 September*

Constantine tells me how happy he was to see you as was my sister-in-law which I already told you. I'm glad that you thought Jeannette's health was better. I see that you are glad to have met her and indeed she's worth knowing. She's very interesting and has a charming personality. I'll tell Helene how struck you were with Pauline's resemblance to her. She'll be thrilled. That young lady has everybody's approval and they say that she is as kind as she is beautiful and good.

## *16 September*

I must thank you, my dear Annette, for your charming gift of two hats and a buckle and I do thank you with all my heart. I will say that those hats are really like you, dear Anne. They are very subtle and they make me very happy but so that the pleasure is complete I must ask you to tell me how I can pay you which I want to do right away. That will make me more comfortable because then I'll feel free to ask you to do my little errands, my dear, without any hesitation. Reading your dear letter sent by courier delights me and so does William's. I must tell you that Louise wrote to Alexandrine and can't praise you enough for your friendship and your sweet and friendly attitude to her. You've made a good impression and, pardon the expression, she thinks you're friendly, pretty and very gracious. She loves your way of talking. So, dear Annette, you've made a conquest and I'm very pleased that you have.

### *Monday 1 October*

You'll be glad to hear of the Empress' safe arrival at Taganrog, my dear. Thank God her health did not suffer from the trip. The Emperor also thinks she's gained strength. It seems that her pulse is less tumultuous. So that is wonderful news. The Empress seems very pleased to be there and even though she was writing me the same day she said that Taganrog had made an agreeable impression on her and that she's very pleased with her accommodations. Anyway, thank God she's settled.

### *Monday 5 October*

It seems to me, dear child, that you're leading a very pleasant life in your charming countryside and that you often meet with very good society. Certainly to be able to see intelligent people and hear good conversation adds considerably to the pleasure of life. The proximity of Tervueren to the city allows you to go to the theatre and certainly as long as they have one there, and that, as at present, the best actors are putting plays on I believe it is most entertaining to go once in awhile. According to the new arrangements here, they tell me that we're keeping the French troupe and that we'll improve on it.

## Gatchina
### *Thursday 8 October*

The Empress tells me that the air is mild, very easy to breathe, so that even the same temperature here that would force us to bundle up warmly, is quite comfortable in Taganrog. She tells me that the sky is very beautiful at night; that the site is charming as nature is so beautiful that the gardens need very little help. The Emperor has already had the wall repaired. He's had the public gardens enlarged and he's bought a large piece of land for a nursery.

The Emperor told me, dear child, that he was charmed to hear that Madame de Wassenaar is staying with you, that you've made a valuable addition on all counts to your entourage; that she's one of those people you love as soon as you know her. He asks me to give you his fond regards. Michael and his wife are in town. They both wrote me yesterday, very happy and quite satisfied in their beautiful palace. Their household is doing well and the young wife is interesting and very sweet. She organizes her time so well. All morning she spends studying in spite of nausea and vomiting. Their little girl is becoming charming. As you want to know the news about her dog and her bears, I'll say the first is all right in its way but I admit I'm afraid of it. The bears, after an affectionate goodbye, were sent to the game park to be cared for. They are becoming very large and important. They had to be muzzled. Now that I've answered your questions, I'll say goodnight.

### *Thursday 22 October*

This evening we all gathered at the round table with our work to listen to *The Siege of Boston* by the American, Fenimore Cooper. I will say that I find him less interesting than the novels of Sir Walter Scott.

### *Friday 26 October*

I'll wait for the first good opportunity to send you your will as you requested. Nonetheless, it distresses me that you're thinking about it now. You should only do that when you're perfectly restored. I received letters from the Emperor dated October 19 from Mohliev on the Dniester. He's very well. Poor Wyley, he was badly hurt in an accident in a carriage, is, thank God, out of danger and won't lose his leg. His loss would have been a real tragedy. His skill is well recognized and he's the only one who knows the Emperor's constitution well. Your brothers, sisters and the Countess send their regards to you.

### Gatchina
### *29 October*

We're presently reading a novel by Cooper called *The Precaution*. I can recommend it. It is very interesting and we enjoyed it. Tell me, dear Annette, what you are reading.

# Chère Annette

Dearest Annette:

I received your letter dated October 15 to 17, our calendar, and will tell you, my dear child, it affected me deeply. Especially reading the expressions you used in speaking of our dearly esteemed Countess. Listen to what I say, my dear, I'm sure you will be sorry and ask that your letter be burned. The Countess is so blind that she can't read or write, indeed, can hardly sign her name. In spite of it all, she maintains a lively interest in those she loves. Her oldest son, seeing the pitiful state of her vision, has devoted himself entirely to her service and is always in attendance on her both here and at Pavolvsk as he will be in town. He's her secretary now and all her letters are dictated to him. She couldn't have anyone more faithful, with more integrity. The Countess is most deeply and tenderly attached to you. The condition she was in when you left, which you won't have forgotten, was again proof of it. Therefore, anything she says to you comes from her unceasing love and caring for you. Never, never would she mean to hurt you and she doesn't even know what irony means. I would never allow myself to speak to her as you ask. It wouldn't be doing you justice because it didn't come from your heart. You've misunderstood her letter. When we were talking about you yesterday (as we always talk about you or your sister every day) I asked her, 'What did you say to Annette, dear Countess, the last time you wrote?' She answered me, but not content to know only from her what she'd written I went to ask her son who acts as her secretary if he remembered what she had dictated. He repeated exactly the same thing. And, my dear, I can't see what is so wounding in those expressions. What she said certainly couldn't be said by anyone other than the woman who raised you, who was a second mother to you, but coming from her, as expressed in her letter, you can't, you mustn't read more than her habit which goes back to your childhood of speaking frankly and with love to you. You mustn't let her language offend you. After all this, dearest Annette, I hope that the misunderstanding has been cleared up and that you will re-establish the friendly relationship which, in all conscience, there should be between you and her. Do you know, dear Annette, that the way you talked about the worthy Countess made me cry. For heaven's sakes, my dear, be fair to her. Remember that at 83 she has twice the right to your consideration, your gratitude and your friendship.

### Tuesday 10 November

Dear Annette:

I've been thinking of you a lot this morning. Duval came to show me two sapphires which are extremely beautiful, especially one of them which surpasses in perfection and depth of colour anything I've yet seen. It's 250 carats, very large and round, the most beautiful colour possible, with an almost magical radiance, cut in the oriental style and it's only 70,000 roubles. The other one is also beautiful but is no comparison to the first. It's 10,000 roubles. It's magnificently set in a circlet of large diamonds. I forgot to ask the price of them as I was most interested in the stone. I know that you and William will be interested in them both especially the first one so I immediately told Duval that I would write to my children and give them a description of what he had shown me.

### Tuesday 17 November

This morning I received some letters from our dear Emperor written on the — of November after he came back from the Crimea. He told me that he's had summer temperatures there but that the beautiful climate is very treacherous because there's a real danger of a chill. The nights are usually very cool.

### Sunday 22 November

There were no presentations today. Our dear Emperor caught a chill in Crimea which bothered him when he returned to Taganrog. These little fevers are very common in Crimea and are not really serious if they're looked after properly.

### 27 November

My children, the most terrible misfortune has overtaken us. Our angel, Alexander, succumbed to his illness which finally affected his nervous system. Even yesterday we hoped for his recovery but heaven wanted to reward a person who is so perfectly good and called him home. He died November 19 at 10.50 in the morning. We received the news this morning. My children, I'm writing you these few lines to say that I am the most sorrowful of mothers but I beg you to bear this misfortune as Christians should. William, dear William, take care of Annette. Annette, my dear, take care of William. Though we weep bitterly let us not reproach providence. The Empress notified me of the cruel news and you can imagine her state. Don't be concerned for me. I'm not suffering physically. God will be our support. Look after yourselves in your grief, for it is your duty, and it will give your unhappy mother some consolation.

## Tuesday 1 December

They say that Petersburg is impressive in its state of profound mourning. There's a general air of silence, of resignation to God's will, of perfect obedience. The churches are full. Here's one of our newspapers which you will weep to read. Translate it to William. Nicholas is much admired by us all. He is wonderful to me as well as to Alexandrine and Helene. We still haven't heard from Michael or Constantine.

## Wednesday 2 December

Oh, my children, what a dreadful position I'm in. What a weight of misfortune afflicts me. May God grant me the strength to bear my trial and complete the sacrifices He intends with acceptance, submission and complete trust in His will. My soul is sick within me but I'm not suffering physically.

## Saturday 5 December

Michael is leaving today to go to our dear Emperor Constantine, and reassure him about my health. He is worried about me. May he soon be here with us. It would greatly soothe my pain. Petersburg is the very picture of sorrow, peace, resignation. The foreigners have nothing but admiration and respect for our excellent nation. Nicholas is like an angel and all my dear children are wonderful to me.

## 14 December

Dear child, dear William, Constantine's wishes were carried out. Yesterday evening Nicholas declared himself Emperor. Chernichef is bringing you the news and should arrive shortly after these few lines are scribbled in haste. The two brothers behaved most admirably and I bless the heavens for having given me such children and I shed tears of gratitude for the divine mercy.

Dearest Alexander. His wishes have been respected. I'm sure that he is blessing his brothers. Goodbye, my dear children, the courier is leaving immediately. My heart is full of emotion but I feel quite well.

## Tuesday 15 December

Dear children, I make haste to write and give you reassuring news. Yesterday morning began with such happy auspices and with tears of compassion and respect for Constantine and Nicholas, it was followed by a frightful afternoon. I had hoped that I had drained the cup of sorrows but we were cruelly afflicted yesterday. Even so, heaven extended its protection over this country and the family because it ensured that those unfortunates who set up the plot and who didn't want to swear an oath of allegiance to Nicholas were just waiting for an excuse to trouble the peace of the nation. Therefore, though they declared themselves as supporters of Constantine, that was only a cover that they used to initiate a revolt. The details will be officially exposed. I just can't go through it all for you. It's too painful. Nicholas was in a most difficult position but he extended his amnesty as long as he could for several hours so that these people had every chance to return to their duty, to obedience. It was only when he saw those who had been misled refusing to listen to the Archbishop who was speaking to them with a cross in his hand that Nicholas ordered the reprisals which were necessary in order to avoid further incalculable harm. Imagine what I suffered, my dear children. I could see the cannon fire from my corner room, knowing that Michael and Nicholas and all the loyal people were exposed to a thousand dangers. A few shots from the cannons put an end to this unhappy revolt and from 8:00 o'clock on everything was peaceful. The rebels only lost six or seven men. All the rest of the guards are outraged but how we mourn the loss of our brave and faithful subjects. Our good, worthy, and excellent Count Melandovitsch, carried away with fervour, was a victim of his loyalty. He was wounded by a pistol shot, the wound was fatal and he died this morning. Other victims fell at the hands of these evildoers who set up and organized the revolt. Those who were drawn into it, and that's the case with the soldiers, are in despair and repentant now. Nicholas has conducted himself with the calmness, prudence and wisdom which would be praiseworthy even in a man of consummate experience. He's also shown himself to be good, great-hearted and magnanimous, pardoning those who were misguided, as was the case with the Battalion of Sailors. The real rebels were all arrested, most of the instigators are, as well, and the plot is being uncovered. Certainly God in His mercy has averted great misfortune from Russia. The people are good and loyal as they usually are. Everybody who was near the Emperor showed their devotion. That's a great consolation to him. The terrible trials we went through yesterday have revealed the virtues of his character but you'll understand how much we've suffered and I'll admit that I'm exhausted with sorrow. Thank God we're all well. Michael has been an absolute angel.

## Monday 21 December

Since my last letter everything has been quiet, thank God. It's quite obvious that the whole thing was a plot set up some time ago which was waiting for an occasion to burst. God clouded their judgement. They've been annihilated for we've arrested them all. The revolt itself will always be deplored but God must have permitted it to expose their intentions. The afternoon was terrible because they opposed the whole family. They planned to take over the palace in order to have the whole family in their power, and, since Nicholas and Michael were both there, if things had gone badly, they would have fallen to the power of the rebels one way or another. In any case, this infernal plot existed only in the minds of a few individuals who are truly enemies of the State or rather vile assassins. As for the soldiers, they were shamefully misled and several young officers who, in fact, belonged to the secret society, didn't see any harm in it because they didn't know what its real aims were. During the revolt, though, they behaved very well. The proof of this is that they were on duty and did exactly as they ought.

## 22 December

I took these [hairs] from the ones the Empress sent me. I believe that I should give you some of them. I've put the best of them in a similar medallion which will never leave me even when I die. I'm also sending you two good engravings. Nicholas is managing like an angel and has everyone's admiration. He's good, kind, merciful and authoritative. His position is very difficult but God, Who's already given him strength for the task, will continue to bless and guide him. Let's all pray for him.

### 23 December

. . . We've lost the happiness of our life and how touching it is to see the high regard all countries had for him. Germany, Holland, France, all give sincere homage which proves how much he was appreciated. These testimonials are dear to my heart as they prove to our angel how well understood and cherished he was.

### 25 December

A dispatch which arrived from Gourief today announces that you know our sorrow and that our dear William told you the news, great God, how he must have suffered, and that you are bearing it as a Christian should, with acceptance, courage and resignation to the will of God. Thank God your health hasn't suffered.

### Tuesday 29 December

I knew that William would be devastated. He's lost a friend, a brother, I'll even say a second father because he loved him truly and very, very tenderly. We hope that William will come. I'll be so glad to see him but what a sad visit it will be, with tears from everybody. It'll be a great consolation to us, though, and indeed we need it. Today we've had the prescribed prayers said for our angel.

### Thursday 31 December

What a terrible year we've just had and under what dark omens the new year is beginning. This waiting period for the mortal remains of our angel is heartbreaking, and I'm also oppressed at the thought of the sorrow that the parents and wives of the people who forgot their duty must be feeling. I pity them from the bottom of my heart. They say there are some very decent women in the families of the conspirators. Unfortunately, I don't know them personally but the pain I feel for them isn't any the less for that.

# 1826

## Tuesday 5 January

Prince William arrived here this morning, exhausted, saddened by our loss – he feels it deeply as he acknowledges gratefully the kindness of the Emperor to him personally as well as the preservation of Prussia which was due to our dear departed's efforts. I was much moved when I saw him. We heard this evening that the dear Emperor's body left Taganrog on 29 December. The Empress attended the service on the 27th. The coffin was closed as it was the day before and also at the church. On the 29th she bid him farewell. She sent news to us that same evening.

## Wednesday evening 6 January

Here I am, my dear child, to give you my kiss and bless you on your birthday tomorrow. May God deign to shower you with every good, especially may He keep you safe and everyone that you cherish, that you love. That is certainly, with no dispute, the most important happiness. May it always be yours. Last year, dear child, I gave you my regards in person and I was so happy. Alexander was with us glowing with health and now, oh, my dear, forgive me, but everything leads me back to that same thought.

## Thursday 7 January

May God bless you, my dear child, may He keep you with every blessing, divine and human. *May He keep safe everyone you love.* If He grants this wish you will be happy. I am sending a gift to you. In the meantime, here is the annual banknote for 10,000 roubles. I have been to the church to pray for you. Many people have congratulated me on your birthday, my dear, wishing you happiness and well-being. I saw poor Wyley today who shed many tears. Empress Elizabeth, who sent me a letter by him, speaks of this worthy person with generosity and real interest, which he deserves, because of his undeviating attachment for our poor angel. He was in despair. Though he saw and felt the danger, our dear Alexander always refused the *proposed* remedies. He counted too much on nature, and, when finally, after receiving communion, he gave in to their prayers and began treatment, it was too late. They begged him on bended knee to apply leeches on the 12th or the 13th but he categorically refused. The leeches would have prevented the blood from going to his head. However, God willed it thus. Our angel was ready for eternity. Yesterday, we had the ceremony of the blessing of the water. There was an enormous crowd and our dear Nicholas finished the ceremony in the middle of the crowd having given orders that his elbows not be held as always used to be done. The crowd watched him with pleasure and greeted him.

## Friday 8 January

The Emperor received the good news that an uprising [at Kiev] caused by the so miserable band which started the explosion here had been put down. The troops behaved marvellously and the leaders were taken. One was killed and the other wounded. They were two brothers; brothers also of Catherine's former maid of honour. I am very sorry for their unhappy father and sister but they are, without any doubt, guilty. Fortunately it is over now and all the trouble spots, except for one, have been taken. Therefore, we must thank God for his innumerable favours in having so obviously kept Russia safe from incalculable misfortune.

## Saturday 9 January

Dearest Annette:

I am distressed beyond words to see how William's departure oppresses and upsets you. I can understand it very well given the season and the emotion which this visit entails. But, dearest child, such difficult circumstances we face. Surely your kind and generous soul must be glad that you can lighten Nicholas' burden and give him some consolation. He says that his reign has brought only trouble. Tell yourself, my dear, that by your temporary sacrifice you will be the first to soothe his heart. He is overwhelmed with business, work. He never goes to bed before 2:00 or 3:00 in the morning. He does not even have the time to have dinner in peace. William's presence will give him new life and do him good. He is thinner, paler, in a way that is frightening. Dearest Annette, think of William's departure from this point of view and, my child, you will temper your regrets with the conviction that you are sending company to the brother who loves you so dearly, more than words can say; the friend and companion of your childhood. Look after your health, dear Annette, and do not make me more unhappy than I already am. I hardly dare tell you the consolation I will feel in seeing dear William. Goodbye, my dear child. Paul has just arrived and I was very pleased to greet him. His appearance has improved and is more poised. I have just seen him briefly. He has gone to make his round of visits now. We have a need to talk out our pain and who can compare with William in this – he is all heart, all tenderness towards us. I will leave to him to tell you of the circumstances. Thank God the evil is known so that, with his protection, everything will be restored. I am sending you an addendum to the account of the uprising. You will see that the unfortunate uprising near Kiev is over and that steps have been taken. The perfidy of several people is frightful. However, it is also consoling to see, as well as these ingrates, people who are entirely devoted to and zealous in the service of the Emperor. Nicholas is taking the best course possible to win general esteem and affection, heaven be blessed. Michael also is behaving angelically. We have great consolation of seeing this so that we can love and honour them both.

Dear Annette, thank you for your dear letter which arrived in the mail. I have already spoken to William as you and the Queen wished about the burial and I will repeat it whenever I can, my dear. I will gather my courage so that I do not upset him. Great heavens, who more than I would wish to spare him pain and avoid everything that could affect his health. Believe me, my dear, his welfare is as dear to me as it is to you. Your dear little angels were so sweet. I will thank them myself. I am going to write a few words to the Queen so I will send you, dear Annette, a most sincere and loving kiss with all my blessings.

## Tuesday 12 January

Count on your old mother, your best friend, to do everything she can to get William to be here before the funeral cortège arrives. Besides which, even if it encounters no obstacles, blizzards and cold snaps, it will not arrive until February 28th at Czarskoeselo and very probably later than that as blizzards are very frequent at this time of the year. The Emperor did not want him to go to the military parade yesterday but they went today. I had the pleasure of seeing him this morning. Then I went to collect him and went to dine with Nicholas who is living at the Hermitage because they are repairing his apartment. We were Nix and his wife, two Williams, Paul and myself. During dinner and in the evening, I was pleased to have William stay a long time with me. We talked a lot. Then about 10:00 he went to see Nix in his office where he enjoyed speaking to his friend. So, you are up-to-date, my dear, on our actions. You will be thinking that the memory of our angel presides over our conversations. I like to talk to William about Alexander because he loved him so well, and he regrets his loss so deeply.

### Friday 15 January

William accompanied Nicholas to the military parade and saw the two regiments of the mounted guards. Then he came to my place. After that, he dined with Nix. I had the pleasure of seeing him in the evening. I have invited the old Princess Golitzene and Madame Apraxin, who he wanted to see. We received your dear letters. I knew how you would feel when you received the news of December 14th. Our hearts were in mourning and will always remember that cruel day. But certainly Divine Providence visited and manifested It's protection of the Empire, the Emperor and all of us. Thank God everything is peaceful and quiet. I have good news from Taganrog. The Empress is well and, God willing, she will remain so.

### Sunday 17 January

My dear child, I feel rather tired this evening. I went to Mass and, as I had to dress in full court mourning, . . . We had dinner as a family at my place. This sight of this hearth surrounded by my children but without the one who brought us all there, gave me a sensation of sadness and emptiness which I cannot express. Dear William feels the same way. He shares my feeling with all the fervour of a loving heart.

### Monday 18 January

I went to the community this morning, my dear, and they were all in mourning. The sight of those charming children with their black aprons moved me deeply. The advanced class feels our loss profoundly. I assure you that everything is peaceful – the public state of mind is excellent and all honest people appreciate and acknowledge Nicholas' distinguished qualities, his noble conduct, his magnanimity and firmness. As soon as he appears the good people welcome him, joyfully and happily. You say that last year you foresaw the storm which broke out. I will admit that nobody here did. Of course, there are always a few hotheads in every country and of no great consequence when they are not influenced by criminals who want the overturning of all order, all rules. Fortunately, they were recognized, found out and are awaiting their punishment. But none of this has any effect on the masses and our national feeling. The most direct proof of what I say, dear Annette, is that in all those grand assemblies you had attended last year, there were perhaps only six of those you might have seen who were involved in the plot and of those, some were only caught up in it through youth and false pretensions. I hope and I expect that, with the help of God, this moment of crisis ensures long years of peace and tranquillity for Russia.

## Tuesday 19 January

William will surely tell you, my dear, the sad ceremony which he saw from the window. The Emperor gave to each of the regiments of the guards the uniform which the late Emperor wore. The two Moscow regiments and the Grenadiers were deprived of this honour because part of these regiments were involved in the December 14th trouble. You will realize, my dear, how moved we were. I could not stay at the window. It seemed to me that this was part of the preparation for the burial and I feel I must protect myself to do my duty on that day. I am very upset today, my dear Annette, and I will not say any more.

## Thursday 21 January

Thank God everything is fine here. Dear Nicholas is truly respected. People are most pleased by his love of work, his goodness and his justice. As soon as he appears people receive him with real joy and apparently more people come to each parade. They approach him with confidence but respect. William will tell you the same. Nicholas works like a condemned man and never goes to bed before 2:00 in the morning.

## *Friday 22 January*

You will be indignant, my dear, when you read the *Journal des Désbats* but you must not be astonished by the madness, even by the lack of good faith. Evildoers cannot believe in virtue. It is beyond their ability. They hunt for the motives of great and noble actions in the murky depths of their own souls where there is only vice, betrayal and intrigue. God forgive them. We must pity them and distrust them. Everything is well with us, my dear. I have noticed, as have the others (we were talking about it with William this evening), that the city is recovering its old activity and it even seems that the people greet us with more warmth. My news from Taganrog is good. They hope that the Empress is improving from what Stofregen and Volkonski write. She tells me that she wants to leave Taganrog if possible in March to be at Tula or Kaluga before Holy Week. That is if spring has arrived and the roads are negotiable or else she will not be able to leave until after Easter. She would like to stay in one of those cities until after the Coronation. I will make my plans to suit hers. When she leaves Taganrog, I will go to stay with her, either at Tula or at Kaluga.

## *Tuesday 26 January*

Everything is quiet and calm here and I believe that Russia will have happiness, peace and security for a long period now. The last of the participants in the December 14th revolt has been arrested – what is more it was in Warsaw where he had fled. He was recognized by a soldier of the Wolynie[?] Regiment who immediately arrested him.

## *Friday 29 January*

My dear, I am sending you a summary which has just been released today in Russian and in French of current events. It will bring you up-to-date, dear Annette, and you will see the undercover, relentless development of the plans of these miserable miscreants and the harm they wanted to do – but at the same time the summary is very reassuring and should put minds at rest about the conduct of the government which was wise, considered, magnanimous and firm. God willing this cruel event, as distressing as it has been, has assured the calm and security of the state since the plot was discovered.

### *Wednesday 3 February*

I send all my good wishes. I also include my gift of 10,000 roubles. I hope you will like the gift which William will bring you from me. I congratulate your dear children on their Mother's Peace Day and press all four to my heart. The family reassures you of their best wishes and their tenderness. The Countess also presents her regards.

### *4 February*

General Trippe has arrived, my dear, with your dear letter. Thank you from the bottom of my heart, dear Annette. I see that your health is better but that your spirit is sad and that distresses me as I can tell how your dear William's absence affects you. I know how each day without him seems empty and drawn out, but I also know that my Annette is capable of the sacrifice and effort on behalf of those who are closest to her. Tell yourself, dear Annette, that especially during these trying times, William's presence here is a daily blessing for Nicholas. A real consolation. He is a true friend with a caring and devoted heart. This strengthens and comforts Nicholas and is of inestimable worth. If you remember that Nicholas owes this happiness to you, it will lessen your pain. Also, dear Annette, think of your poor mother. I need so much comforting and William has been helpful, so sweet to me. No one knew our dear angel better than he – his great qualities and all the goodness of his character, the charm of his close friendship. So no one understands my grief as well as he does. We are one in our regrets, our sorrow, and his presence is an inestimable balm for my poor heart. Tell yourself that everyday I say to myself, 'Annette has given me this consolation,' and you will have the satisfaction of knowing that you ease my pain. Dearest Annette, I beg of you to look on William's temporary absence in that light.

### *Wednesday 10 February*

Everything is peaceful here and, please God, we will soon be at the end of this horrible plot whose discovery assures, I hope, a calm and happy reign for my son. We still have some terrible times ahead of us, especially when our angel's mortal remains arrive here and we pay him our last duty. I have put my trust in God, my dear, telling myself that since we have borne his loss we can bear anything. The news from the Empress Elizabeth is good. She has accepted Oranienbaum and its domains which the Emperor has given her as being the particular property of the late Emperor. He also gave her Camenienstrof but she did not want to accept it. Since Nicholas told her, though, that he would always consider it to be hers, she gave it to Michael. As well, the Emperor endowed the Empress Elizabeth with a million in revenue. She did not want to accept any more than the 600,000 which the law allows her but since Nicholas said that the other 400,000 would be held in trust for her anyway, she has just said that she will put it to the upkeep of Camenienstrof which must be close to that sum so that Michael will not have that responsibility. This summer she will live outside Moscow, I think on Prince Volkonski's estate because we found that [place] which was to be arranged for her was humid and prone to cause fevers because of the lakes. We still do not know her intentions for next winter. It must be painful to her to come back to Petersburg. I am more aware of that than anybody else. The fact that she is still alive is a miracle of faith. Certainly life has its share of sorrow.

### *Wednesday 16 February*

My dear child, I received your last letter dated 1/13 February with feelings that I find difficult to express. I see that you are distressed, anxious, afflicted and, allow me to point out, unjust towards me for you seem to accuse me of not doing what you and the Queen asked in requesting dear William to leave us before the painful duties we now face. You are wrong, my dear. I did suggest an early departure right away and have repeated the suggestion as has Nicholas. But you know how sensitive William is. The idea of duty is supreme law to him. He believes, as he lives, that it is his duty, or at least by taking part, he can prove to Russia the great affection of that of a brother, even a son, that he had for Alexander. He told me that if he left before the ceremony he would forever reproach himself, and be unhappy with his conduct in this and that his fears for me, for Nicholas, indeed for all of us, would be much more difficult to bear and more dangerous to his system than the emotion which could fill us with despair, even moderate, as we have a mutual duty to support each other's courage. Dear child, this is what he said. I will even tell you that I have consulted the doctors who say that as he feels so deeply it would be better for him to fulfil these duties rather than to avoid them and that is the exact truth.

## *Thursday 18 February*

The Duke of Wellington arrived this evening. He will have his audience tomorrow. William is pleased to see his friend, Lord Somerset, who lost an arm in the Battle of Waterloo. Their meeting makes William very happy.

## *Friday 19 February*

The Duke of Wellington had his audiences today. I think he has lost weight but he still has his beautiful features and he made me very happy by what he said about our dear angel, and about Nicholas whose conduct on December 14th he much admired.

## *Thursday 11 March*

This is a sad day for me, my dear child. You will be thinking about me; you will be praying with me for your worthy father. Now, he is reunited with the son he loved so well from childhood on and surely they are both praying for us.

## *Friday 19 March*

What a wonderful memory used to be associated with this date and how unhappy I am today when he is no longer here. Dear Anne, we will never, never be reconciled to the loss of our angel: this benefactor of humanity. There is a big parade today. The Emperor will distribute the medals which Alexander had intended to give out today and which have not yet been distributed. The parade is also in honour of the Duke of Wellington who is going to leave us soon. I am sorry and I am especially upset that circumstances deprived me of the pleasure of seeing him much. He spent the evening with our family for the first time. His conversation is so interesting, there is so much sense in everything he says and his manner is so natural that he puts everyone at ease. The more one sees of him the more one would like to see of him. The weather is good for the parade and I am delighted for Nicholas' sake. God be with him in everything. Everything is calm and peaceful here. Public spirit is high. Nicholas captivates the public opinion in the capital and in the provinces. His hard work in the business of the nation pleases the people. He is just and firm. Please assure the King and Queen of my regard. My compliments to the Prince and Princess Frederick and to Princess Marianne.

## 20 March

Helene is going to leave for Moscow after the 25th so that she will arrive before the end of her eighth month. I intend to start, after April 21st, to arrive in Moscow at the end of April. Helene is due somewhere between the 1st and the 10th or 12th of May. However, if the Empress Elizabeth arrives at Kaluga before then, I will go to her. That is what is planned as God wills.

## Friday 9 April

You reproach me, my dear, and I do not think I have deserved it. I believe that I was acting for the best – we all did – wishing to spare you pain in not telling you of the dates and the heart-rending ceremonies. At least recognize our good intentions and do not be unjust. It gives me such pain. I hope that William is near you and that you are content and happy.

## Kaluga
### 1 May

I have been here for an hour, my dear, and hasten to let you know that I am expecting the Empress tomorrow night, or the morning of the next day. It will be a dreadful meeting. God give me courage. The welcome I receive everywhere, dear child, has moved me deeply. It really seems that our misfortunes have only increased the affection of the people. Their expression on seeing me is so contented that I cannot tell you. Then tears come to their eyes when my deep mourning reminds them of our dear Alexander. Heaven be blessed for the devotion of our excellent people to the sovereign and his family.

## Beledo
### 5 May

God has sent us another sad trial which deeply distresses me but we must bear it with acceptance and resignation. I would let William know. The details are painful. I am well, my dear. Heaven sends me the strength to do my duty.

[Letter enclosed to Anna Pavlovna.]

Already the great concern about the hopeless condition of Her Majesty, Kaiserine Elizabeth, has naturally seriously disturbed the spirit of Her Majesty's mother who was informed of the matter on her arrival in Kaluga on May 1st by the Doctors Strofregen and Prince Volkonski; especially as it was announced May 3rd that the 'noble invalid' because of her great weakness had to stay in Belov where she had arrived with great trouble and had the greatest wish to see the Kaiserine. All the more distressing was the impression made by the news that the suffering of Her Majesty on the journey inland to Belov had come to an end ('in death') at the Station Podborka. Meantime I can reassure Your Royal Highness about the condition of her mother, Her Majesty, the Kaiserine, that Her Majesty has withstood this very sad event (thank heaven) with Christian composure. That she doesn't suffer physically and that I have reason to be completely satisfied with her health.

J. Rechl
Moscow, May 8, 1826

### Sunday 16 May

We have sung a Te Deum, my dear, for Helene's safe delivery and Elisa's birth. I would have liked you and William, dear Anne, to enjoy with me the magnificent view of the Kremlin filled with people, all the amphitheatres built for the Coronation filled with spectators, keeping silent and quiet. After the Mass and Te Deum, shouts of hurrah broke out and followed me to Michael's house. The people moved me with their expressions of attachment, contentment and the goodwill on every face. The nation is wonderful and I would be more than ungrateful if I were not deeply moved by their feeling for the dear departed, for Nicholas, for the family, for myself. May God keep them always. I am tired out by the heat – the ceremony lasted two hours. Helene has milk fever. She has been suffering post-natal cramps which aggravates her nerves. But everything is going well.

### Moscow
### 27 May

I arrived late yesterday evening, my dear Annette, so I could not write. I needed to rest. It was very hot and naturally emotion was high. I hope to attend the burial of the Empress, intending to leave here on the 15th, to arrive on the 20th or 21st. The funeral should be on the 23rd, that's the date that was set. The baptism was to be on May 30th, next Sunday, and Michael intended to leave that same evening to arrive in time for the signing of the investigation but a courier arrived after dinner today with a letter from the Emperor that he should receive the report of the investigations on the 30th. Therefore, Michael's presence is necessary and the baptism can be rescheduled for his return which might be the 14th or the 15th. My son begs me not to make the trip to the burial as I would be risking my own health. He requests and begs me to give up that plan.

### Thursday 3 June

The heat is terrible and it is so dry, dear Annette, that we are all drained. After visiting Helene, I went to get a breath of air in the country on an estate of Aide-de-Camp, General Lesonofski[?], which is outside the city on the banks of the Moskva. On the left there is all Moscow before one's eyes and on the right is the countryside. Truly, the country around Moscow is very beautiful. As for Moscow itself, it is magnificent, imposing, really breathtaking.

### Sunday 13 June

Thank God, my dear, the baptism is over. You will realize how trying it was for me to be there in the Kremlin where our Angel so much liked to be, where I enjoyed being because I often had the pleasure of seeing him there. His apartments were above mine so he could come down the private staircase without appearing in public. Yesterday evening was difficult, my dear, very sad, because of all the heartbreaking memories and the trying awakening. However, I had to collect myself and the baptism helped me. Everything went off very well. There was a dinner for the first three classes but there was no music because of the court mourning. The toasts were made to the sound of cannon fire, drums, trumpets, and the ringing of the bells. It was really impressive.

### Monday 14 June

The cortège [of The Empress Elizabeth] is entering Petersburg. These are going to be days of long suffering. God help the Emperor and the Empress.

The heat is oppressive. It is hard for me to be unable to take part in this sad duty with them and I will always regret it. I attended the funeral Mass and prayers this morning and so was able to share in the feelings of this day.

## *Monday 21 June*

It is a day of mourning, of regrets, of cruel memories. How sorry I am for Nicholas and Alexandrine but how much I regret not taking part in their duties today. I am extremely sorry, I have not left my house all day. This evening I went around the garden. The weather is so beautiful and the air so pleasant. My God, how beautiful Moscow is and how I wish you knew this lovely city. Tell William that I am thinking of him a lot and remember with pleasure his enthusiasm for our old capital.

## Melaitze
### *2 July*

As we were leaving Moscow, my dear, I received the letters which you sent by courier as well as the lovely gift you sent me for my feast day. Thank you, my dear, the watch is very pretty and gives me great pleasure. Your promptness in doing this for me heightens its value in my eyes, as nothing is more dear or precious to me than evidences of my children's tenderness and affection. I will wear this lovely watch often, my dear, always grateful to you. The contents of your letter made me very happy. I see that you are content, well, pleased with your stay and having found the King's leg almost better. I hope most sincerely that it will soon be completely cured. The Queen will have been very pleased to see her brother, Prince William, and her excellent sister-in-law. She is one of the most beautiful women I have ever seen and is also intelligent and good. Your lifestyle seems very pleasant to me, my dear. Without any doubt, it is the power of nature, though, that has the most charm for me.

## *13 July*

A courier from the Emperor tells me that the rebels are to be executed today. The Emperor has mitigated the death penalty of 24 others to hard labour. He has not sentenced anyone to death. The five who are to be executed he delivered to the Supreme Court for judgement. This news, which made me thank God for Nicholas' mercy, nevertheless caused me such emotion that I was flooded in tears. May God have pity on them and grant them repentance and a Christian death.

## Moscow
### *16 July*

Letters from the Emperor dated the 13th, received at 10:00 in the morning here, tell me that everything was done with perfect calm and order. Many of the rebels showed their ill will even on this occasion. Nix wrote me a few words of reassurance. Thank God it is over and heaven willing we will now dare hope for a happy reign for poor Nicholas who has experienced so much trouble.

### *Saturday 17 July*

Tell William that Tchernichef arrived with all the details of this horrible affair. Several of the guilty men prayed for the Emperor just before they died. I am sure that God will grant them grace. Dear Anne, let us bless God that everything was peaceful and that it is over. Volkonski's son was stripped of his rank and had his sword broken over his head. He is condemned to hard labour. He merited the death penalty. I cannot say any more, my dear. I have to receive people and I have only a few minutes to dress. Tomorrow we are putting our mourning aside for the Coronation, so no more black paper, no more black suits.

## At the Kremlin the evening after the entry
### *25 July*

We had the Grand Entry, my dear, and it was superb. I am sure that William would have approved of the way the city looked, magnificent. The crowd was enormous and the weather superb. Everything was in perfect order and everyone was pleased to see Nicholas here. The day was splendid but very hot and I will admit that I am tired.

### *Friday 30 July*

Our weather is still magnificent and I try to take advantage of the fresh air by working on my terrace. The view from here is unbelievable – it must be the most magnificent anywhere. It's incredibly expansive, including all the surrounding area. Moscow is delightful. The Empress is well. Nicholas, too. There was a great review which went very well. Sasha was with his regiment and went past before his father, riding his fat horse at a gallop with the rest of the troop. He is like a little angel, perfectly at ease, noticing everything without any false embarrassment. His father was so thrilled and the troop and the officers were enchanted with this charming child.

## The Kremlin
### *1 August*

I wish, my dear Annette, that you had been with your family today as well as our beloved William. You would have enjoyed the wonderful spectacle which we had in front of us. You know, dear Annette, that there is the blessing of the water on this day, therefore, we have this ceremony. The Emperor, me and Helene went with the procession which left from the Convent of Tchendova[?]. The guards who accompanied the flags which had been blessed were all in a row and commanded by Michael. We crossed the whole square of the Kremlin, went down the ramp to the quay where there was a tent. The clergy came right down to the water. The crowd was enormous. All the amphitheatres, prepared for the Coronation, were filled with people. An enormous crowd was on the ramparts and on the opposite bank. The most beautiful sun shone on the ceremony; the weather was heavenly. Calm silence and perfect order made the ceremony more regal. It was truly majestic. By its beauty and its position, Moscow gives religious ceremonies a dignity unknown to Petersburg. All foreign observers were lost in admiration and, indeed, there was enough to marvel at. It was very hot but beside the river there was a refreshing breeze.

## From the Romanofski house
### *12 August*

I attended the examination at Alexander's Institute. I had every right to be pleased with them. The Institute is very worthy. The children are well cared for, well equipped and healthy looking. The houses are well built and the location is delightful. I spent an evening in this lovely house where I was even tempted to take some exercise in the garden.

## *Friday 13 August*

Today, dear Annette, I have been out a lot. I went to the Kremlin to see Nix who works there until 1:00. Then I went to the other end of the city to meet Paul at the hospital which I was glad to show him and he was very pleased with it. Then I took him to the Golitzene Hospital which is a magnificent establishment and which Prince Serge has made even more wonderful by adding a hospice for the infirm. It is marvellous to see such an establishment founded and maintained by a single person. Nicholas was very happy with it and truly the two establishments are beautiful. Then I went to have tea with Alexandrine who is very well. It seems to me that she is putting on weight. After staying with her a while, I left to return home. The distances, though, are enormous.

## *15 August*

Dear William and you, my dear Anne, will share our satisfaction in seeing our dear Costa here with us. I cannot express strongly enough what I feel but my whole being is filled with gratitude to God for protecting me and granting my wishes. You cannot imagine the happiness, the enthusiasm which Constantine's arrival causes here. People make the sign of the cross, bless themselves, and now say that all the lies that plagued us are put to rest. The crowd at the parade was enormous. We went to the Cathedral of Uspenski as it was their Feast Day and I must say I have never seen a more beautiful sight than the Square covered with people whose expressions were all contented. It was wonderful. The magnificent weather further embellished the scene. We had dinner with Nix and this evening Costa stayed with me until midnight and talked. My heart was filled with joy and I was very touched by his confidence in me.

## *Wednesday 18 August*

I had very little time to myself. Since Costa is here for such a short time I am keeping as much time free for him as possible. Costa will be his brother's assistant, just as he was at Alexander's Coronation. Michael will also be with them. That is perfect and it is all because of Costa's good and noble conduct. God bless him.

### Saturday 21 August

Pray for Nix, my dear, and you, too, my dear William, pray for him. I am going to write to William today. Imagine, both of you, what I am thinking of and ask heaven to grant me courage and strength. My dear Annette, the Coronation went very well and was extremely solemn. Constantine was sublime and earned the veneration of everybody for his fine, noble conduct which united regret to the most tender, brotherly affection for Nix and Alexandrine. Thank heaven Alexandrine bore the fatigue well. Nix was very handsome. I am so full of emotion, thanking God for having given me such beautiful children.

### Moscow
### Thursday 26 August

I am sure, my dear Annette, that you have been thinking of us a lot. I will tell you what we have done day by day since I know the details interest you. Nicholas and Alexandrine held a formal audience at which they received the congratulations of the Emperor's household, of the guard, of the officers of the army corps assembled here, of the court, of the nobility, of the different provinces of the Empire, of the fourth class, the mayors of the 40 odd provinces and all the gentlemen of the region. This took a long time because Alexandrine had to have rest periods. I have to do the same thing tomorrow and then I will have fulfilled my duties on this occasion. Celebrations are no longer part of my responsibilities. I will attend the one which the Emperor gives the people, though, as otherwise they might be surprised if they did not see that I shared their pleasure.

### Tuesday 31 August

Fifty years ago today, my dear Annette, I arrived at Czarskoeselo between 6:00 and 7:00 in the evening, August 31, 1776. It was a hallmark in my life. I thank God for my blessings from the bottom of my heart, for His generosity, and for His support during the cruel times I have also experienced. It is one year today, at this same hour, between 6:00 and 7:00 in the evening, that I bid farewell forever to my dearly beloved Alexander and that I blessed and held him for the last time. Dear Anne, you know my suffering. I attended prayers for the dead this evening and I beg you to excuse me for today.

## *14 September*

Nicholas received the news that our ambassador to Persia, Prince Menchikof, who was detained at Erivian, has crossed our borders with all his retinue. The Persian showed great perfidy in launching an attack on us when our ambassador was actually in their country. They will be thoroughly punished but it is sad to have to do it and to have to sacrifice our men because of the disloyalty and betrayal of these people. We were anxious for Prince Menchikof when he was held at Erivian but fortunately he and his retinue were already at Tiflis. Heaven grant that Nix will have the happiness of seeing this episode soon settled and peace and tranquillity re-established. Our farewell audiences start today. Monsieur de Steding[?] has had his but I will see him again at the dinner which I am giving the ambassadors tomorrow. That is the only thing I have been able to do to honour them during their stay as I am living now in retreat. We had a grand farewell dinner for the marshals of the nobility and the mayors of all the provincial capitals who were delegated to attend the Coronation and who are now returning home.

## *Wednesday 15 September*

Tell me, dear Anne, are there still many foreigners in Brussels? Here they are soon going to leave us and Petersburg will seem quite empty after the great affluence of people. Nicholas has received only testimonials of love, affection, attachment. It is heartwarming to see the welcome everybody gives us. The way they salute us when we are out in the carriage and how they hurry to see us. May God keep the people so contented. The dinner for the diplomats was very successful.

## *Thursday 16 September*

The celebration for the people was superb. There were *more than* 100,000 people there. The Square was decorated and our salon was round and in the middle of the sea of people. A table for more than 40,000 guests was laid. Fountains of brandy, wine and beer were set out in the Square which was decorated with different galleries for the spectators. There were carousels, theatres, slides, see-saws to amuse the people. The weather was cool but it was not raining. We left at noon and returned about 2:00. The rest of the day I spent working. This evening I went to see the room which Countess Orloff has built for tomorrow's celebration. It is very beautiful. My dear Annette, I must finish this letter adding only a few words to ask you to accept these trifles from our factories. They are really prospering and I hope you will find these things well made. I will be pleased to know if you will wear them out of patriotism.

## Tuesday 21 September

I have come back from a trip of 50 versts which I made to the estate of Prince Peter Volkonski. This is the place Furbonov[?] where the Empress Elizabeth intended to spend the summer and which the Prince had arranged for her with a care which showed his attachment. Everything was done to Alexander's taste and style. These little attentions were still there, even to his favourite sofa. The Empress had the sofa which the Emperor used to lie on during the first days of his illness moved there from Taganrog. You can imagine what impression the sight of it made on me. His writing table was there, too.

## Monday 27 September

My congratulations, my dear, on the news which Nicholas has just received of General Paskevitch's victory over the Persians. He has completely defeated Abbos Mynfa who was the one who crossed our borders near Elisabethpoli. He captured three flags, three cannons, 1,000 prisoners, 80 boxes of powder, two senior officers. As Nix tells me, a complete victory. So these evildoers are punished for their disloyalty. We will have a Te Deum sung tomorrow. It is a good start which, God willing, will soon end the war which was started by this vile treason.

## Thursday 30 September

The Emperor and Empress met me this morning at 10:00, my dear Annette. We all went to Prince Yousoupof's beautiful state of Archangelskoi which I believe you know. It compares to those lovely places outside of Rome in style of building, the proportion of the rooms and the profusion of paintings and marble which is found there. The garden is magnificent. The Moskva curves around and embellishes the estate.

### *Monday 18 October*

Our weather is terrible, dear Annette, but I went out in the carriage. Nicholas' generosity has made Pavlovsk more beautiful yet. He has kindly given me, as a present, on July 22, some iron gates of the most wonderful design and beautiful proportions. He made sure it was in place for October 14th. It adds another charm to the entrance of Pavlovsk. He also had the Avenue of Lindens paved, which will mean an end to all that dust. It is a charming enhancement which is, of course, appreciated but the fact that Nicholas wanted to please me really warms by heart and he was completely successful in that. I have given the gate his name. I did not dare put an inscription on it because his modesty would be offended but he cannot refuse the tribute of the name. Pavlovsk seems to be well maintained and cared for.

## St Petersburg
### *Tuesday 19 October*

Here I am back in town, my dear. The dear Countess bore the trip well. She feels fine, only a bit tired. I found my children all in good health. We all spent the evening together except for Nix who had come earlier to talk to me for an hour. He is working very hard and everybody appreciates it. I received your letter, my dear Annette. You reproach me for not having answered what you said in letter 110. I did not forget, my dear, but I have not done it yet because I know what a heart you have and that you would not want to cause pain. I told myself that you would regret it if I carried that matter to Nicholas for it would not settle anything. But a formal complaint by the Grand Duchess to her brother, the Emperor, becomes such a serious matter that I wanted to give you time to reflect on it. Besides that, my dear, letter 110 expresses your dissatisfaction in general terms without any specifics. If you have facts and can give me all the details and circumstances, and if you still wish that I *formally* notify the Emperor, then please tell me so. But, dear Annette, I must warn you that Nicholas does not take things lightly and you would be exposing these people to disgrace which I am sure you do not want to do. It would lower our esteem in the opinion of our countrymen who are accustomed to think of the members of the family as protectors. Besides, my dear, remember that everybody in the mission was approved by you and William. If by chance somebody has offended you, I would expect it was inadvertently or through lack of attention for it is certainly in their interests to accord you the respect, submission and consideration due you on three counts – your noble birth, as sister of the Emperor, and as wife of William. However, my dear, I will speak to Nicholas if you still want me to but in that case send me the detailed facts.

## Saturday 23 October

Dear Annette, I have just seen the woman who used to be your waiting woman. She tells me she is happy and content. She feels herself very fortunate. She is very conscious of your generosity, telling me, 'The Grand Duchess has done more for me than I have heard of or expected.' She is very grateful. She is overweight but well. She said you, as well as William, are held in great affection, attachment, respect in Holland, in Brussels, in the whole country. She told me of the great good you do. You can imagine, my dear, how I rejoiced to hear this even though I have known it all for a long time.

## Saturday 13 November

They have just brought me the box with the two charming bonnets which you kindly sent me. They are very pretty and I will think of you when I wear them, dear Annette. Would you believe, my dear, that at 11:00 a.m. the Anglican bishop has already been presented to me along with the other ministers of this Protestant religion. There were eleven or thirteen. Then I saw some other gentlemen who were also presented. I see by your last letter, and thank you a thousand times for it, how pleased you were with the alacrity that the States General and the people in Brussels showed in coming to see you and give you homage. These sentiments are very pleasing.

## Sunday 14 November

You will be happy to hear, my dear Annette, that pretty Marie's future is decided on. She has agreed to marry Prince Charles the 1/13 of November. She is pleased, quite happy with the prince and the little girl as well as the grandparents and the father. The King and the prospective bridegroom are very pleased. I thank God for the future happiness of these dear children – Charles' kind and good character seems to guarantee it. He is very much in love with her and has been faithful. Dear, kind Prince William came with his brother. In spite of all the painful memories which oppressed him and which he must have felt, he did not want to refuse the King's and Prince Charles' request. They say he was very moved. Marie was touched by his feelings. You can imagine how Marie must have felt but she is well and seems very happy, thank God.

### Wednesday 17 November

My thoughts are taken up with cruel memories. One year ago today I received my last letter from our Angel in which he picked up a bit of fever in the Crimea and at that date he was already at death's door. That is what is terrible in separations – a few days makes all the difference – even between life and death. I am sorry, my dear, for mentioning these sad memories but my heart is overflowing.

### Sunday 21 November

The courier to Brussels is leaving at 9:00 this evening so I am writing, my dear child, to thank you for your dear letters. I see that you, too, are preoccupied with memories of our beloved Alexander, paying him that tribute of sorrow. He will live for ever in our hearts, and in the memory of those who respect virtue, value, good deeds and who are capable of gratitude. The day of his death was a day generally mourned and I am sure the sorrow was the same everywhere in the country. I see, my dear, that the thought of attending the ball on the 6th is upsetting you. However, since it is part of your duty to the Queen, you cannot, indeed, must not miss it. Though it taxes your spirit knowing that we are still in mourning here, you know that our angel approves of what you do. William writes that he does not intend to leave the country until after the 19th so, as the period of mourning will then be over, you can be a little easier about fulfilling your social duties which in your position must be observed, dear Annette, and which you also do so well. But I know you will be sorry to leave your charming country estate and I suppose that, even in winter, you will often go there on sunny days for an outing. Michael asks me to convey his love to you, dear Annette. He is overwhelmed with work and hardly has time to eat or sleep but that does not affect his spirits which are very good. I believe

Helene is writing. News from Marie is good. She seems contented and quite happy with Prince Charles' character. He must be very much in love with her. God grant this dear girl happiness.

## 26 November

I must thank you, my dear, for your letter of the 7th to the 10th and I am glad to hear that you have returned to the country to rest after the fatigue of the celebrations. However, I see that you enjoyed the day and were touched by the friendliness and goodness of the King and Queen. Their affection for you is as dear to me as it is to you because it matches, to a degree, our affection for William. He makes you happy and heaven, in granting you such charming children, has blessed you both. Enjoy your good fortune, dear Annette, for as long as you live. That is my special prayer for you. You should have received the payment for the year, dear child.

## Sunday 28 November

Your two brothers are well, dear Annette. I saw Nik yesterday morning. He is very well. He is putting on weight which suits him wonderfully. I spoke to him about a chapel master to lead your cantors. He will speak to Prince Volkonski and I will hear the result of their inquiries when I get into town. Today, Michael came to dine with me. He was in sparkling humour and puns and jokes followed apace. He is very good at it. He left quite late. We spent the afternoon talking and that very seriously.

## Saturday 4 December

I also reminded him [Nicholas] of his promise of the portrait of Michael and one of himself. Michael asks me to tell you, dear Annette, that you are too fair to be angry with him for not writing for truly he does not go to bed until 12:30, 1:00 and starts work again at 6:00 in the morning. He often does not dine until 5:30. In fact, I do not ever see him for more than a little while as he is overloaded with things to do. Here is the account of your capital. I reproached Villanof for the omission you accused him of but Mons Schultz' letter in March only mentioned the delay in the bank notes for 25,000 roubles and said nothing about your capital so our reproaches were unjust as he proved to me. Here are the notes from the cabinet for the September trimester. From now on they will not be late.

### *Wednesday 8 December*

It is so dark, my dear child, that I can hardly see what I am writing. At least this is the shortest day and the sun will soon return. We have not had any winter yet this year. The river is open, therefore no sleigh transportation across the ice. It is a real calamity especially when the supplies should be brought in for Christmas. However, since the seasons usually arrive on schedule here, I do not despair of seeing winter in a few days. It is certainly to be wished for.

### *Friday 10 December*

I hope I will soon be able to tell you of a choice of a good chapel master for your cantors, and I am even pleased to tell you that I had intended to engage him for a position in Moscow (he was a cantor at court), but the place you have offered is more advantageous for him and he is anxious to take it. So, I will give him up to you quite happily because you will have gained a good person. Perhaps it will all be arranged by Tuesday.

### *Saturday 11 December*

Today is the anniversary of our first meeting with dear William. I can still see him coming into my room with our dear Alexander. I can see you there beside the keyboard in my study. I see it all right before my eyes. Only the person who arranged your happiness, whose image is facing me and who I often contemplate when I am writing you, can no longer enjoy seeing your happiness but he will live in our hearts for ever and ever. The lack of snow and ice makes it difficult to bring in supplies for Christmas. The river is not frozen over yet. That has never happened before.

### *Tuesday 14 December*

This is a date of such conflicting feelings. God's protection was with Nicholas, the Empire and all of us when that frightful plot was uncovered and when we were also shown the attachments, zeal and devotion of so many people. Though our gratitude to them is unlimited, it is terrible that such an event could ever have happened and that the rebels caused the misery of their family and the shedding of blood. You can imagine, my dears, what I am going through. We went to Nix's chapel where he had gathered his aides-de-camp who had shown such zeal, devotion and loyalty and we heard the Te Deum. We all felt the same way and thanked God together for saving the state, the Emperor and, indeed, all of us.

## Wednesday 15 December

I thank God for waking this morning to a very different state of affairs than this time last year. Let us thank God for having re-established the old order, peaceful and calm. I have even found that the people show us more affection and attachment than before. I read an article in the gazettes from Brussels. I have copied it and include it because I am asking you, dear Annette, to tell me what you think and to find out from Dr Everaert what he thinks about these operations. If they are effective and give back hearing to the deaf and dumb, I want to know the means and all the necessary details. Co-operate in this good work, dear Annette. I will be most obliged. I have just seen that your school for girls, using the co-operative approach which you have sponsored, is prospering and has grown to 120 students. Teach them also to work with linen and tell me what work do they do? Please tell me these details. Here is the name of the cantor who is leaving for Brussels: Luof, who replaced Bartnovski, praises him and says he is well qualified to conduct and guide your chapel. He has a bass voice and knows music very well.

## Saturday 25 December

Congratulations on this Feast Day, dear Annette, and William and the children. There is a grand procession and the Emperor inaugurates the Great Hall which he built between the White Hall and the Hall of St George. They are going to sing the — after the usual Te Deum sung at church. We will be going out early so I must hurry to get ready. . . .

## Wednesday 29 December

The Academy of Sciences is celebrating its centennial and has invited all of us. We are going there in half an hour, my dear, and maybe you will be interested to know, dear Annette, that 50 years ago I attended a similar celebration for their 50th anniversary with your worthy father. Unfortunately none of the academicians from that time is still alive, dear Annette. You see, my dear, we are going to honour science as it deserves. The sciences are necessary and are the glory of the nations which encourage them.

# *1827*

## *Sunday 2 January*

Yesterday's masquerade must have been beautiful, dear Annette, and the location superb. Having given dinner to my family in my study at the Tauride, I saw the arrangement of the rooms and gardens which were decorated with the most beautiful flowers; especially at this season they delight the eye. The decoration of the hall is as you saw it and as it was for Michael's wedding. I left the Tauride after dinner and spent my evening working and being read to.

## *Tuesday 4 January*

I knew that your evening would be a great success. You preside beautifully and you entertain so well that, of course, people are grateful for such a warm and friendly welcome. I am sure that the Russian delegation felt the same way and I beg you, dear Annette, in generosity and justice to believe me. How could it be otherwise! Do you intend to give soirées with dancing, my dear, and when will they start? I suppose that the entertainments at The Hermitage will begin very soon. They certainly give a great deal of pleasure.

## *Saturday 7 January*

Here is the note for 10,000 roubles which you will be pleased to accept, my dear. All the family congratulates you, and the Princess [Lieven] joins her good wishes to ours. I am sure William and the family will give you a wonderful day.

## *Sunday 8 January*

There was a production at The Hermitage this evening. They put on *The Spouse of the White Woman* by Boldieu. I did not want to tell you yesterday of something very sad that happened here yesterday morning. Poor Gagarin, who was in my service, had been ill for many years and had fallen into a black melancholy with continual anxiety and agitation. It made us afraid for his sanity. Yesterday morning, he got up, had breakfast with his wife and spent a long time in prayer. Then he went to his room, sent the servant on an errand, and cut his throat, severing the artery. I was very upset and am very sorry. There was a lot of good in him. He had a fiery temperament and could get carried away but he was good hearted and of noble character with all the abilities necessary for court life. My dear Annette, according to our dear old customs, I am sending you my good wishes and blessings on the eve of your birthday. It has been two years since I have had the pleasure of giving them to you in person. I will always cherish that time together. But even though we are apart, my good wishes are as loving, so you know that I want you to have every spiritual and temporal blessing, all the happiness possible in this world. God keep you and everybody dear to you. I hope I may, God willing, have the joy of seeing you again. We went to Mass accompanying the procession right to the stairs. The Emperor and Michael and the flags followed and we watched the ceremony from the Empress' study, the one in the corner nearest the Admiralty. My children took up residence in their apartments yesterday but they wanted me to see them in daylight. They are very attractive and the Emperor's apartment on the third floor is really magnificent in the beauty and size of the rooms, the view and the simple, elegant furnishings. The apartments of the Emperor are now much more convenient. The bedroom is very beautiful. It is in the same place but the bed has been moved. The dressing room is charming and the corner room has been made into a study which will be delightful in the spring. The furniture is mahogany and lovely. The late Emperor's big cabinet is now a bookcase with red and yellow curtains. It is a very handsome piece of furniture. The blue room is very well arranged. The salon where the Emperor has heard Mass is decorated with a beautiful tapestry and, as an ornament, there is an enormous malichite baths which William would appreciate. The corner room, which used to be the chapel, is hung with a superb yellow material, of gold colour. The woodwork, the furniture, the ornaments, everything is very attractive. The library has ornamental vases of jade and porphyry and two Tintorettoes, one the Hebe which you saw at The Hermitage, decorate the study in the corner. The Empress also has a charming little study on the third floor so that she can be closer to the Emperor. It is delightful. The wood is straw coloured like one of my rooms at Czarskoeselo. Good taste is evident in all the furnishings. Not too much gilding. The salons are beautiful and rich looking. The rest is elegant. The Emperor and the Empress seem well pleased. Nicholas told me that he definitely intended to send you a letter by this courier and I am taking this opportunity to send you my gift, dear Annette. I sincerely hope you like it. I hope you will, and if you do, I will be completely pleased. It is the first piece of the tiara set with turquoise which I had promised you and so that you can see the effect better I have included, with your birthday present, another piece for your name day. I will add to it all, God willing, in the coming years. In the meantime you can wear it as it is by adding two bands to set it in. I have the impression that it will suit you marvellously and William will think it is lovely, that my dear Annette will be pleased with my taste. I am also including the note from the Lombards which is for both amounts, that for your birthday and for your name day. This is such a good opportunity that I have made good use of it. I am pleased to hear that the Queen is stronger and feeling better. I am very fond of her. It is fortunate for you, too, dear Annette, that the King's health has improved because his survival influences William's happiness and yours. In this century, the highest position in the land is not one to bring happiness. How good you are, my dear child, to ease your sister-in-law's loneliness by your friendship and kind efforts. It seems that her husband, the Prince, is very busy with work which takes all his time but it is trying for a young woman and especially difficult to be left so much alone at the beginning of a marriage. That is never a problem in the family home of a young Princess for she is always surrounded by the people responsible for her education. I hope she soon becomes a mother for then she would have something sweet to interest and occupy her. Does not Princess Marianne spend much time with her? And is there any discussion of a marriage for Princess Marianne? There certainly are not many princes right now. How did matters stand with the Electress of Hesse? Is there a reconciliation with the Elector or not? Her situation is very difficult. The testimonials and affection which you received, dear, gladden my heart and are proof of the esteem and goodwill which you have earned. I can swear, my child, that I have never heard of any Russian who has travelled say that you are not loved in Brussels. On the contrary, I have heard how popular you are. I have certainly not heard any mention of your pride, nor of the diamonds you wear. I have never known you to be proud and as for the diamonds, your position requires that you wear the ornaments that you have received. Believe me, my dear, that criticism is not worth listening to even if it is being said, and I doubt that it is.

It may even have been invented by those who are jealous of the Russians. I am sure, my dear, that everything that has been repeated to you would have sounded quite different in context for how could the Russians not be supportive of you? For heaven's sake, banish the thought that you are rejected by your compatriots out of your mind. You do an injustice in believing it and it must distress you. No, my dear Annette, you are loved and cherished by your Fatherland. The interest shown in everything you do should assure you of that and as for that, my dear, Russia has more affection for the family of its sovereign than is the case in other countries. People may talk indiscreetly here, as they do everywhere, but at the least incident all the idle words disappear and the nature of their true sentiments is obvious. I can do none other than approve your good and loyal feelings about what true Christianity means, that it always preaches forbearance and indulgence. When I need to remember it I always think of our Angel, who was such a good example in every situation. I hope, dear Anne, that you may be happier with the family's diligence in writing to you, as I see by what you tell me, that you have received letters from Helene. Nicholas has assured me that he wants to write you today. Michael is so busy that I often do not see him until midnight. He hardly has time to breathe. I have reminded him of his promise of a portrait as well as reminding Helene that she promised hers, seated in her study. I see, dear Anne, that you are learning the Dutch language. That is well done and will really please the country. I see by your latest letters, dear Anne, that the bank notes for the September term have arrived. From the time of the first Grand Duchess' marriage it has been the custom of Cabinet to pay out for the January trimester in May, the May trimester in September and the September trimester in January. That is how all of Cabinet's payments are arranged. You wanted to receive the September trimester payment before the end of the term and it has been arranged that way since then. Now you want the Hope Institution to take over these payments in May, September and December. I am sure that Cabinet will make the payments precisely when they are due. Therefore, I must ask you, my dear, whether you persist in wanting to receive them from the Hope firm. If this is so, I will pass it on but, if you want my opinion, I believe it would be better not to change a custom which has been established for such a long time. Only the most unfortunate circumstances, such as the death of the Emperor, the death of Count Gourief, and the interval between Cabinets were serious enough to cause a delay and it will not happen again. However, you let me know, my dear, what I have to do, what you want me to do, and I will carry out your wishes. You tell me with delight of your outings, dear Annette. I just think of the beautiful parks in Brussels and I can imagine your pleasure. I was sure, dear child, that your ball would be a marvellous success. I am looking forward to the ones you will give in your new house. They will be superb there. When do you think you will be able to take up residence? Thank you for wearing the turquoises. They suit you so well and I expect that the part of the tiara which I am presenting you will look wonderful on you. I am telling you that I can hardly wait to hear that you like it. Your cantor is completing his last arrangements before he leaves and will soon be on his way. That will be another opportunity to write you. Everything is fine, thank God. Nicholas is working very hard. People are very pleased with his decisions and diligence. He has an enormous work load. Michael has a lot to do, too. In fact, has not a minute for himself. Helene, poor dear, is vomiting. There is not much doubt about her condition and it is beginning to be noticeable. Nix's children are well and charming. Michael's oldest daughter is very delicate but seems better these last few days. The younger girl is an angel of beauty, gaiety and sweetness. Alexandrine must always be very careful of her health. She is very thin. I hope that the country and the good fresh air will give her back her strength and put a little weight on her. Without ever being sick, she has never been quite well since last spring and it is only natural after everything we have gone through. The Princess is well. She sends her congratulations, her regards for your birthday. You will be happy at the length of this letter which I finish with a fine kiss and many, many blessings.

### Tuesday 25 January

My morning was taken up by two trips to our schools where the awards were distributed to the children. These schools are very successful and the work which they do there is useful and very pretty. The first class are making their trousseau, colours on white, often on linen or satin (patinelle and satinelle) which they do very well. They also make gloves. All of our instructors are excellent. I can only congratulate myself on their devotion to their duty. They are very pleasant to me. I had dinner with several people and I will tell you as an item of news that I have finally decided to give in to Nicholas' wishes and what they all say, and have my rooms redone. The furniture is in shreds. They will be in the same place but two towers added to the area of the rooms which my household occupied, enlarge my dressing room and my little study so that I will be able to have a bedroom there. When the plan is finalized, I will send you a copy. They finally convinced me to have it done.

## Friday 28 January

Congratulations on Michael's birthday. God keep him safe. He is a very distinguished person, worthy of our love and affection. The Emperor is celebrating the day with a ball for 500 to 600 people which will be held in the rooms adjoining his apartment, the same place where our dear angel used to give them. Supper will be in the large room where we usually have it on December 12th. The beautiful apartments of the Empress will be open. Everybody is excited about this ball, and, though I will be in my rooms, I share the general satisfaction. Many thanks for your dear letter and the details you have given about your gifts. The pearl must be superb and I congratulate you. Pearls are truly charming to wear. The plant stand also sounds very lovely. Won't you send me a drawing of it? You will be glad to know, my dear Annette, that Constantine arrived here this afternoon, taking us all by surprise. Grabovski had told me in the morning that Constantine was at Strelna but I thought it was just a rumour. There are often such rumours which our information seems to verify so our hopes were high and there was great joy in seeing our beloved Constantine. He took four days to get to Strelna and then gave himself the time to have a good night's sleep, to rest a little, to take care of some business which had come up on the way, and then he came here. Entering the palace revived painful memories for him. Fortunately things have been changed around and he saw Nicholas in the new apartments. We spent the afternoon and evening together.

## Thursday 10 February

From what the family tells me, yesterday's masquerade must have been one of the best ever. There were 32,000 tickets distributed and about 24,000 came in. They said that though there has never been such an enormous crowd, there was perfect order. It is reassuring and an honour to the nation to know such gatherings can take place at the palace without disorder or inconvenience. Everybody must have been anxious to see Nicholas. We are happy to have this opportunity. The family came to have tea with me during the masquerade. Constantine spent the evening with me as he did not go for the reasons I told you in my previous letters.

## 15 February

I am sending these few lines with your cantor, my dear, who leaves tomorrow. He waited until there was a boat from Memel. He told me it will take him nearly 30 days to get there so, dear Annette, I am only sending a letter of recommendation with him. He has promised to make every effort to deserve your kindness. They say he is a good subject and a good musician. The cantor said he would do all he can to arrive before Holy Week. Today is Mardi Gras, dear Annette, so I suppose all Brussels is alive.

## Good Friday 1 April

I expect, dear Annette, that you will have thought of proceedings today and that the memory of the *tristesse* still makes you feel the sadness. Your last letter pleased me a great deal. Thank you for all the details about your trip to Tervueren and your various outings and especially for the *sample* of spring which you sent to me. Dear William told me that your oldest son has broken out in a rash like smallpox. We have it here, too. It is an eruption which resembles smallpox but is not. It is as rare for a person who has been vaccinated to get smallpox as it is for someone who has been inoculated. It does happen, but it is a real break-down of nature and the doctors seem to think that if we understood smallpox better, we would be able to eliminate sickness. That would be a great benefit to humanity.

## Easter Sunday 3 April

*Xpucmocb bockpech*, dear Annette. I send you a kiss of blessing and congratulations and rejoice that we celebrated the Feast Day on the same day. I hope you spent it pleasantly. The religious ceremony was very beautiful. There was a crowd there. The service of congratulations lasted three hours. Thank God I supported it well. The afternoon was brilliant: slides, see-saws, all sorts of games were set up in the castle square and along the boulevard. The square was therefore very lively and the people are really happy with the location. They see that the Emperor loves them as he wants to see them celebrate.

## *Easter Tuesday 5 April*

Finally we can settle back into our usual calm routine, my dear. For the past three days there has been a parade in front of the Emperor's windows. There was a crowd and the sight of all these people, of the wonderful troops, of all the amusements placed along the boulevards and on the square of the palace, really is like a wonderland, especially as we have had most brilliant beautiful weather.

## *Friday 9 April*

Dear Anne, please get Madame Kent to attend to this letter. I am asking her for lace for Alexandrine's and Helene's layettes. I would appreciate it if you would look after sending it. If it is well wrapped it could be sent to me through the mail, to my address, under your seal.

## *Friday 15 April*

This morning I went around to my conservatories. Many beautiful plants are blooming and my collection is very interesting. Nonetheless, such a walk is tiring and hot. However, this evening I had tea in the beautiful conservatory of orange trees. We spent the evening reading. We are reading a novel by Walter Scott's rival. It is *The Last of the Mohicans* by Cooper. I must admit I do not find it interesting for the work is rather contrived, events are stacked upon each other and very violent and cruel.

## *Sunday 18 April*

I have received your letters of the 8th and 12th of April and thank you. I really appreciate what you are doing, dear Annette, in arranging for the arrears due the Invalids and the Patriotic Women's Society to be paid. It is like you, my Annette, your good heart and your sense of justice. I will be sorry though, my dear, if, in your letter to Validof cancelling future payments, you give the reason that those two establishments have not claimed both payments. They could not do so because they have no written engagement to put forward. I pay my share each year but the institutions have nothing which could authorize them to claim those sums from me. If you give that as your reason, I imagine you will get an answer to that effect. I gave the list for the payment of the pensions for people you named to Monsieur de Validof right away. I must also tell you that I did not give him any order to cancel those payments in time. When you gave me the report in February that these persons had not yet claimed them, I told him that in that case, wait a little longer because you will receive instructions from my daughter. I can see that you are upset and annoyed as you say, dear Annette, to know that your Englishwoman had to leave her apartment in the palace. This was a general measure, my dear, and extended to the maids who are maids of honour as well as anybody else who was living in the palace without working there. It was necessary because people who were in active service could not be lodged in the palace. In the time of the late Emperor, the only people who lived there were himself and the late Empress and Michael. Now, the family includes four children and we are expecting a fifth, so the number of people has increased. Besides, dear Annette, the Emperor gives a housing allowance to all these people. A wardrobe mistress, who was in my service and married to a valet to your late father, also had to leave the palace as well as Marie's chambermaids. So, my dear Annette, this was a necessary move and, for mercy's sake, do not imagine any other motive. I will always be very happy to see your Englishwoman and do her service.

## Tuesday 19 April

When I got up I saw the earth, roofs, covered with snow and an unbearable wind blowing. This is after we have had stifling heat. That will bring on colds and chills in great numbers. I was so indignant with the weather that I did not leave the house but amused myself by having people in to dinner. This season is *recalcitrant* and gives the most disagreeable sensation. Then I remembered something the Count d'Anstadt[?] here during the time of the late Empress Catherine . . . [he] often said, 'We have to take the weather as it comes and them as they are.' According to this maxim, we must resign ourselves to our cold weather.

## Monday 25 April

This morning I saw a portrait of our late beloved Alexander on horseback. It is very like him and stirred my soul. Since the weather was superb I went to Gelaghin this afternoon and saw the place where I kissed him for the last time. How can I tell you what I felt, what I suffered, the cruel memories. I went to Camenienstrof to see his rooms and those of the late Empress. Michael has kept everything in Alexander's quarters just as he left it: handkerchief, spectacles, everything is in its place. It seems that he will soon be back and when one realizes that he has left us for ever, your heart aches and a profound sorrow overwhelms you.

## Wednesday 27 April

Nicholas has seen that your Englishwoman received 1,460 roubles as a living allowance and that 600 roubles had been added for lodging since she left the palace. He has just added another 400 roubles, so she will receive a living allowance of 1,000 roubles. You see, Annette, how willing Nix is to make you happy.

## Tuesday 10 May

It might be right at this moment that I am writing to you that my poor Marie must part with her child. All my thoughts are with her today and I can almost believe I see the sadness. I have gone through it myself so I know how she feels. I walked to the Elisabeth Pavilion by the lower path today and came back on the opposite bank, again on the lower path. The view was wonderful. The greenery is so fresh and so lavish that I could not stop looking at this charming valley. We will have a profusion of lilacs and that is when Pavlovski is at its best. As I walked I heard a nightingale singing. The lilacs are budding and there will be wonderful show.

## Thursday 26 May

Thank God, Mutterchen is better. She is still very low, keeping to her bed, but she has less pain and fever. She has some appetite and her mind is clear but we have a long way to go until she recovers. Let us hope that heaven will bless the doctor's efforts as it has until now. Nicholas came to see me. He is going to review the fleet. He really wanted me to be there but he understands that Mutterchen's condition keeps me by her bed.

## Pavlovsk

### *31 May*

You tell me, my dear child, of the unsuitable conduct of the diplomatic corps at Count Gourief's ball. It was perfectly stupid and senseless. Nicholas feels the same way and has admonished those responsible. Several courts have blamed their ministers and disavowed them and I do not suppose that Mr Canning will approve the behaviour of Lord Bagot. He is too intelligent and sensible to let it pass. I am astonished that Lord Bagot, who we supposed to be an intelligent and proper man, allowed himself to be involved in such a false, unreasonable undertaking. Dear Nicholas acted as he always does, as a good brother and as a sovereign who commands respect. You always behave most properly so there can be no complaint of your conduct. Just continue as customary. If Prince Frederick gives greater latitude in his receptions, I suppose, as he is the second son, his circumstances are somewhat different and not of the same consequence. That is how I explain it to myself, my dear, as I cannot allow myself any other interpretation given my distance from things. You tell me, my dear, that I have not answered several points in your letters. I thought I had. I do remember that I did not answer one topic: the one where you complained of Louise. But before I had the opportunity of being able to answer in confidence I received letters from you in which you praised and seemed very pleased with her, so I thought that everything was cleared up and that you understood each other. I rejoiced wholeheartedly and believed that it would be indelicate to bring it up again. Rest assured, dear Annette, that everything that affects you concerns me and that my constant interest is in you for life. I will leave it there for today. I must thank you, dear child, for your last letter and the information you promised me on the culture and preparation of linen. I know that the Port of Riga was sending some seeds to Holland and that the linen prepared under surveillance from that seed is finer than ours which must come from how it is processed. You will be doing me a great service in giving the information of the procedures used which give these good results. I see that your oldest son already dines at court. Little Alexander also appeared for the first time at my dinner on May 21st. He is developing the most advantageous way and so are his sisters, and as for Oline, she is an angel. I have never seen such a sweet child so fine natured and kind as that little darling. She knows how to make herself loved, gentle and yet so gay. She is not at all beautiful but everyone loves her for her goodness.

### *Monday 13 June*

I congratulate your dear children for their success in shooting. William's ingenuous astonishment when he was applauded omens well for his character. I expect that this little triumph, however, pleased you a great deal. We like to see our children succeed so much that the smallest thing which shows some talent appeals to our maternal pride.

## Gelaghin
### *16 June*

The countryside of Brussels is delightful and gets more beautiful every year due to the care taken in cultivating it. I see, dear child, that the art of painting is not fostered as successfully in your country as it once was. It seems to be the same in every country with the exception of Rome which must have some good painters.

### *20 June*

I saw an assembly of more then 2,000 young people, dear Annette. The Emperor convened all the corps of cadets to the camp. He was good enough to give them two superb dinners in tents yesterday and today. We went to the one today. Young Alexander did the honours Saturday evening. Sasha marched with his company of the cadet corps – dressed as they were, carrying his supplies on his back and his gun on his shoulder. . . . He was not at all tired even though it was six versts. He was very happy and very proud of his company. He is a charming child, well endowed by nature, who gives us great hope for the future. There is no better character and he is developing well in every respect. The sight of this great number of youths, all destined for the services, is very inspiring. May heaven protect them and grant them all success.

### *Sunday 26 June*

My day was tiring, my dear. First there was an audience for Lord Mitford. Then I gave a dinner to almost one hundred people and the evening was spent in the Rose Pavilion playing cards while the young people played their little games. As I become unaccustomed to people and the demands of society, I am exhausted, so I am going to bed as soon as possible. The dear Princess took a step today from her bed to her chair without support. She did not lift her leg. She was happy and I was even happier. Tomorrow is her birthday – God keep her.

## *Monday 27 June*

I was at Czarskoeselo to see the ceremony of the English ambassador's audience in which he presented the Order of the Garter to the Emperor. The ceremony was very impressive. The mantle of the Order is a superb colour. Nicholas looked very grand during the ceremony. We saw him through a curtain where we had had several slips made.

## Czarskoeselo
### *1 July*

I am enchanted by all the details that you have given me on the sweetness of your little girl. She must be very appealing. I would eat her up with caresses if I had the pleasure of seeing her. What is she like with her Papa and brothers? Yes, my dear, the dangerous, even fatal condition of mother preoccupies me. A tie of forty years standing, which more than thirty years have been spent devoting herself and all her cares to my children, give her a sacred right to my gratitude, to my veneration, to my friendship, and we all feel this way. Her condition is a cause of general sorrow for us and the closest concern of the public to pay her [Princess Lieven] the just tribute of affection.

## *Friday 22 July*

My day was very long – I'd never seen Czarskoeselo more sparkling, busier than this evening. The Emperor brought a hundred young cadets from the camp at Czarskoeselo and these dear, young people played on the bars set up on the lawn. Sasha is as agile as a little monkey. The little girls were in the adjoining reception room with the children of all the people who live here and at Czarskoeselo. They had dancing; there was a crowd in the garden; the weather was good; everything was most festive. When I returned I found a crowd here in the alleys and in a square of the castle. I went right away to see the princess who was well. After staying with her for a while I went across the courtyard of the palace on foot to please these good people who had waited for me for so many hours.

## Tuesday 2 August

When I was about to go to bed last night I received a letter from Nix who was kind enough to send me word that General Paskevitsch's aide-de-camp had brought in the good news of a victory over *Abbas Nirza*. The result was the surrender of *Aban-Abad* (near Araz). The trophies of the day were the keys of the city, full flags, one of which was *Abbas Nirza's* and his son captured with two of the pages. This should have had good consequences. Our losses have been nothing in comparison with the gains. We lost two officers and had some men wounded. The Te Deum will be sung at the Palace of the Tauride on the 5th.

## Monday 8 August

I see, my dear Annette, that your entourage, as well as the King, the Queen and Her ladies were kind enough to remember Mother's Day. Please tell them how grateful I am. I am especially touched that the Queen, in spite of her suffering, thought of me. Her friendship is dear and precious and I sincerely return it. You are astonished, my dear, that the legation didn't come to congratulate me. It's surely due to the absence of the minister and a lack of competence in his staff.

## Camenienstrof
### 16 August

My dear Annette:
Heaven has given you a beautiful little niece who was born to dear Helene this morning at 8:30, as easy a delivery as possible, most happily. Michael welcomed his third daughter in the nicest way. We thank God that everything went so well and beg Him to grant the same favour to Alexandrine. The baby is named Catherine which makes me very happy. Poor Michael has strained or rather twisted his foot which has caused him some pain yesterday and today. However, given the occasion, he is hobbling about with a cane. Congratulations, dear Annette, on the anniversary of the coronation of Nix

and Alexandrine. God bless them both and grant the Empress a happy delivery. Helene was so fortunate. She could not be better. I heard Mass with my family at Gelaghin. I returned there for dinner and in the evening I went out with Alexandrine in the open carriage during the public promenade of the island. Nicholas and Michael were on horseback. There were a lot of people and touching enthusiasm and great gaiety. There were an astonishing number of carriages in perfect order. The whole island was open. There were a quantity of groups of musicians, singers, acrobats. It was all very lively. At 8:00 we went in and from the house we watched the fireworks display put on by the city. Then I went to see Helene and returned to my place, rather tired.

### Friday 26 August

This morning I attended the most regal and touching ceremony. The Emperor is going to have the triumphal arch, which was erected temporarily in 1814 on the Peterhof Road to welcome back Alexander and the Guards, reconstructed as a permanent monument. He assembled all the Guards who fought the campaign of 1812 to 1814. They made a camp of more than 8,000 men, all having been decorated, having deserved it of their country. In the presence of this élite company, a crowd of people, we laid the first stone. You know that involves religious ceremony. When the prayers were finished the Emperor asked me to place the first stone in memory of the late Emperor to whom Russia owes her glory and her triumphs. You can imagine how this touching and kind attention of Nicholas' affected me. Next, the Emperor laid a stone for himself and his wife. I then placed mine and young Sasha and Michael theirs. The religious ceremony ended with the Te Deum in memory of the late Emperor.

### Friday 9 September

Heaven has given us a son, my dear Annette. Alexandrine gave birth, very easily, to a baby boy this morning at 3:30. He is strong, healthy and well nourished. You will imagine, my dear, how happy we all are. It is times like these that make life a pleasure and which remind me of all I owe to my children in that regard. Everybody was transported. Happiness radiated from Alexandrine and Nicholas, who was crying with emotion. The dear child was given the name of Constantine. It is a name which our dear Constantine has made forever illustrious in the annals of Russia. After the Te Deum, I received all the congratulations and Nix and I dined together very late. Then I went to Camenienstrof to see dearest Helene who rejoices with us.

## *14 September*

Mr Fischer is just bringing me a collection of double dahlias gathered from the Botanical Garden. They are superb in beauty, variety of colour and size. He has a wonderful establishment and his collection of plants is magnificent. It is remarkable how well the flowers are lasting this autumn. I have also gathered the most beautiful double roses just two days ago at Gelaghin. The dahlias are still in good condition. I have never seen them more beautiful or more varied in colour, better shaped and doubled. They ornament the garden and, *en masse*, they make a wonderful effect. Tell me a little about your garden, dear Annette. Helene's forty days of confinement ends the day after tomorrow and she looks fresh and beautiful. The new born child is a pretty baby and doing well. The second child is superb but the oldest is still weak and feeble. It is so sad to see a child in that condition, however, the doctors have hope for her. Nix's children are extremely well and developing quickly. Young Alexander is the most remarkable child and so are the little girls. The two oldest apply themselves and are very sweet. Oline is the joy of the household by her sweetness and good nature. I have never seen a more delightful child, nicer or better, there is no [child] that is so charming. Little Constantine is well.

## *13 October*

My dear Anne. I am confident that you and William will have been thinking of your old mother, praying for her and recommending her to God's care. I was heaped with testimonials of love and affection from my children. Nicholas gave me a superb vase which is priceless in my eyes because when our beloved Angel was at Catherinenbourg he saw it being made and himself took a hand in it, working one of the leaves sculpted on the vase. Nix also gave me a Saint Cecilia, beautiful and really delightful with two beautiful emeralds, one sapphire and two rubies. It is very handsome – too handsome for me. That is what I told Nicholas but he answered that it distressed him to hear me speak that way. Alexandrine gave me a beautiful inkwell of malachite made in a completely new style with two malachite vases. These things, and the vase that Nicholas gave me, are for my new rooms.

## *Monday 17 October*

I hear the same old Annette speaking as we used to in the good old days when she was still in the family home. Always keep to these principles and heaven will bless you for it. You combine feeling, reason and calm reflection and what sweeter joy or consummation for a mother's heart than to see you becoming more and more established in such noble ways of feeling and acting. Nix was extremely happy with your letter, my dear child. It gave him great pleasure and reminded him vividly of the good old days of triopathie. I was really touched to see how happy he was.

## *Tuesday 18 October*

I was very happy to see Countess Voronzof and talked a lot about you, my dear. She was very pleased to see you and to find you surrounded by your children. She says your boys are very handsome, very well brought up, and your little girl is delightful – charming, gay, very happy with a doll her brothers had brought her and very funny when she was cross at her Papa for calling her Mademoiselle d'Orange. She tells me that this little one speaks so well, so prettily, arranging her words so well – in all, she is a little angel and it is charming to see you with your children around you. The day she spent with you and William was delightful.

## *Saturday 22 October*

By the way, dear Annette, the gazettes say that you and William have been invited to Paris. Is that true? This trip will be for William, complement of the good work he did at St Omer, a trip which had the best possible effect and for you, my dear child, it will be very interesting to make personal acquaintance of the royal family, especially of the dauphine. It can only strengthen the ties of friendship. Besides, I know that Annette will delight in seeing all the masterpieces of art and science which are collected in Paris and which you will appreciate. This thought gladdens my heart because you will enjoy it so much.

### *23 October*

I congratulate you, my dear, on the surrender of Erivian which happened October 1st/13th, the feast day of the Blessed Virgin. I beg you, my Annette, to tell William who will certainly share in our satisfaction. Dear Nicholas will be very happy and pleased. In previous wars, Erivan had always been able to resist the efforts made to take it. This time, after a five day siege, they breached the walls and even though our troops were in the fortress, through the breach, there was no looting. Perfect order was maintained and the famous Hassan Pasha, the right hand of the sovereign, was taken prisoner as well as the garrison. Thank God our losses were light. It was a beautiful deed of arms, glorious for the troops, from a military and a moral point of view. I hope it has good results.

### *Sunday 6 November*

Received news by indirect route of a great maritime battle in the Bay of Navarino and the complete destruction of the Turkish fleet. We will have to see if it is confirmed.

### *Monday 7 November*

The Emperor received confirmation of yesterday's news through Florence. The English admiral had told the minister at his Court. He described it in these words: 'The conduct of the Russian and French admirals *was admirable.*' The Turkish fleet was destroyed. They were the first to fire on the negotiators, one of whom was even killed so battle was joined. This was an action without good faith or law on the part of the Turks and they must suffer the consequences. We are waiting for a courier to arrive any time now.

### *Tuesday 8 November*

As the Turks committed the disloyalty of killing the two negotiators and fired the first cannon shots, battle was engaged and the victory was complete. Thanks to God, the Russian squadron, under Count Heyden's command, suffered less than the others and will continue to patrol the sea. Ibrahim Pascha had already broken the armistice in embarking his troops to ravage the Peloponnese. Their conduct is most profoundly disloyal because it contradicts the general opinion of the Turkish character which, until now, was that they honoured their word. The destruction of their fleet is their punishment. The Emperor has not heard from Constantinople since this news reached them. This evening Nicholas wrote me a note to tell me that he just received the news by courier that *Tauris* surrendered to our army without any difficulty. We took 31 cannons, 9 mortar and the famous Alazar Hon.[?] It was our troops who had to prevent the people from looting the castle. They welcomed us as liberators. Tell me about this pavilion that the King gave the Queen. Does it have a garden around it or is it just a belvedere? I beg you, my dear, when you look at the sea strain your eyes as far as you can to try and find us here on our shore.

### Thursday 8 December

You make me laugh, my dear, in giving me the reason you are interested in the fall of the Ottoman Empire. I do not feel the cold as you do but I hope that moderation on the part of the Turks will dispense with any worry that we might have had about that and I will hope so. Do you know, dear Anne, that I am astonished at how many people there are at The Hague? I am judging by the amount of presentations you have received. Tell me, then, are all these people established at The Hague or do they only come occasionally?

### Thursday 15 December

I am charmed that your concert succeeded. Marie was also enchanted with Mademoiselle Sontag's talent. She must have been very well educated and she conducts herself very well in society. I am glad to see, my dear, that you are cultivating your taste in music. It is a charming pastime, as is drawing. Do you still do any? It would be too bad to abandon it when you are so skilled. I am happy to see that William is interested in the concerts. Often, as is the case with him, this is a taste which develops as one grows older.

### Friday 23 December

We are expecting news at any moment of the signing of peace with the Persians and, thank heaven, everything seems to have ended well there.

Nothing has yet been decided from Constantinople. The three ministers have left but peace is not confirmed. We will have to trust providence that all will end well.

## Sunday 25 December

I am sending you my offering, dear Annette. It is the continuation of the turquoise tiara. Once again, I have given the gifts for your birthday and your name day together so that you will have them earlier. Let me know, my dear, if they join, if not, please send me a measure of how much is missing so that it will encircle your head. I will be very happy if this little gift pleases you. I think the tiara must suit you. Duval has indicated how to join it.

# *1828*

## *Monday 2 January*

I want to tell you more about yesterday's masquerade, my dear. There were a lot of people, about 16,000, but the crowd was larger last year. The cold this year kept many people away. Today is just as cold so everybody is staying in their own quarters. The temperature is devastating. We have not had anything like it for many years. Yesterday, to go to Mass, we passed through the new external apartments which have been decorated with taste and magnificence, especially the old oval salon where we used to dance and which is called the service room and the Emperor's throne room which is now most beautiful. It is furnished in crushed velvet with bronze eagles. The throne is magnificent and the decorations are superb. The oval salon is also very beautiful. The columns have been gilded and the ceiling has been painted in a tasteful style. In general the palace has been much improved in condition, cleanliness and magnificence. My interior apartments are charming.

## *Thursday 12 January*

I see, dear Annette, that you still like flowers and that, like me, you decorate your rooms with them. At the present time, we have already many hyacinths, camellias, lilacs, — and, as you call them, innocent tulips. I have found that ivy does very well in the rooms and I have decorated two windows with it. I see that you have received my letter of December 11–14 where I tell you how pleased we are by the request the King asked of Nix which will mean that William will come here. I am sure you are as anxious to see me again as I am to see you. *You say that you cannot say anything definite yet* but that you will write when you have the opportunity. I hope there is one soon. The circumstances seem to favour the possibility. I gave your letter to Nicholas, my dear, and he says that to send a courier directly to The Hague at this moment would give rise to gossip and speculation which must be avoided. The couriers from London can carry any packets. I advise you, my dear, to have a letter ready so that you do not have to write in a hurry when the courier passes. Right now, the minister cannot even say when they are going as it depends on the circumstances. Therefore, my dear, write ahead of time so that we will know your intentions as soon as possible.

## *Sunday 15 January*

Dear Annette, I went to The Hermitage where the Italian troupe appeared for the first time. They put on the *Barber of Seville*, music by Rossini. The men are very good; the prima donna leaves a lot to be desired, maybe she'll improve.

## *Thursday 19 January*

The ball I gave this evening to celebrate your birthday, which has just passed, was beautiful – very sparkling and lively. Mr de Heeckeren was invited and seated at the table with the Empress. Our dear Nicholas and Michael and the others who have been decorated with the Order of the King wore it at the ball. Apparently it was the eve of your sister-in-law's birthday so we gave our congratulations to Mr de Heeckeren. I told him that you had spoken to me very feelingly about the kind attention of the King and the Queen and the family coming to congratulate you on the Russian new year and that you always count yourself fortunate in having their friendship and the kindness of the King and Queen and the friendship of the family. It seemed to me that Heeckeren was pleased. We wish him well here. He is very proper and pleasant.

## *Thursday 26 January*

Share our satisfaction, my dear Annette. Beloved Constantine arrived this afternoon, in good health, vigour and disposition. The happiness of having him with us is great and his presence is always enjoyed. Constantine's special inheritance is a truly distinguished character and so many beautiful and noble memories that one heart is not enough to love and cherish him as he deserves. He is in such good form that he wanted to go to the entertainment at The Hermitage with us and had supper with me, eating with good appetite.

## *Sunday 29 January*

I slept for an hour this afternoon. This evening there was an Italian entertainment at The Hermitage, *Cinderella* by Rossini. Though the music was beautiful, I preferred *The Barber of Seville* and *The Robber Magpie*.

## *Tuesday 7 February*

Dear Constantine left today after supper and I am sorry to see him go. He only comes once a year and it is sad to be apart so long. God guide him. He was very pleasant, very gay. May God keep him. He is certainly a very, very remarkable person.

## *Sunday 12 February*

But dear Annette, you are unfair to Nicholas and you insult the special feeling of the *triopathy* which you valued so highly in one of your recent letters. You told me to tell him this. I did so because I know that he loves you dearly and he would not believe that you needed a letter with his signature on it to tell you that he would be delighted to see you. My letters say it for all of us. For if you reread the first letter, you see that it is Nicholas who brought me the good news. He then asked me to express our happiness that William was coming and the kind intention of the King and I wrote you immediately. Let this persuade and convince you, my dear, and believe me that our only wish is to match yours. That is all we want, my dear, and do not be unfair to poor Nix; he is so overwhelmed with business that he has to work into the night to keep up with it all.

## *Monday 13 February*

I am very grateful, my dear, for your letter of January 29th to 31st. You tell me so sweetly, so pleasantly, of the little adventures of your three sons that I laughed with you but, at the same time, I thanked God that the oldest boy's bayonet did not go in his eye, that Alexander's fall was not serious and that little Henry's sore cheek was not an ulcer. It seemed that I could see the little girl hovering around her brothers. She must be very sweet. Will you not send me her portrait?

### *Tuesday 14 February*

They told me that a courier is being sent in haste to England and that he will go through Brussels where letters can be forwarded to The Hague. So, I am writing, my dear, as I have some time to myself. Our public horizon is darkening in the east and the Turks are extremely insolent. Their kind of manifesto upsets and offends all Christian powers and combines insolence to the most striking bad faith and stupidity. It is devastating to have to admit and expect that there will be war. Nicholas must stop all his good work in the daily running of the country which has already had such good effect on the public welfare. I cannot give you any official news about Persia as the snow has made communications difficult.

### *Friday 17 February*

The cold is insupportable and still lasts. It is devastating because it paralyses everything. This has been a very Russian winter. The peasants are happy as they say that it assures us a good year for the crops. I do not think that garden enthusiasts are of the same opinion. I fear for my plantations. I was interested to read in the gazettes details of the exposition of flowers and plants at Gand. The effect must have been ravishing.

### *24 February*

Dear Annette, weep for our beloved Princess [Lieven] who drew her last breath this afternoon at 5:45. We have lost in her a mother and friend who was truly worthy of our respect. She lived for us, so let us pay her the tribute of our tears and regrets. There is general mourning. I am well, dear Anne, but profoundly stricken. Great God, what a death! A saint could not have gone without acceptance, peace, faith and love for us all.

### *Tuesday 6 March*

My dear child, I am sending the music I promised. Here is a collection of our best marches. Do play them with all the more pleasure in learning that it is dear Nix who gathered and arranged them.

### *Friday 9 March*

. . . however, this morning our dear Nicholas received the news that peace with Persia was signed February 9th at midnight. A messenger brought the first news of it. The courier who brought it is due here imminently. Thank God for this. It is an essential benefit in the circumstances.

### *Friday 16 March*

It seems to me that your stay at The Hague has been more lively this year than usual and that you have enjoyed it more, which I am very glad to see as it is as it should be. My dear Annette, the Emperor is giving a formal dinner today to mark the peace. General Paskevitsch received the title of Count of Erivian and a gift of one million roubles. All the other rewards to the military are also generous and worthy of Nicholas who knows how to appreciate merit.

### *29 March*

I hasten, my dear child, to tell you that William has arrived in good health, that he looks very well and that he was greeted with joy and happiness. We were all thinking of you, dear Annette. I received the charming pictures of your children. Those of the boys resemble the ones I already have. The one of your little girl is delightful. I think she looks like you, dear Annette, and William tells me that she is even better than her picture.

## St Petersburg
### *Sunday 1 April*

We spent part of the morning watching the departure of the Sappers of the Guard and the Sailors of the Guard who are on their way to the borders. You can imagine, my dear, what I felt, especially as I know your brothers are leaving at the end of the month. We went to see the Ismailovski Regiment at the finish in victory leave. William thought they looked wonderful but it is a sad sight for the wives and mothers. The troops marched out confidently. God bring them back without loss. I still sometimes persuade myself that the sultan will be considerate. Seeing the danger that threatens him, he may — . God, let it be true. Nothing else to tell you.

---

### *Monday, 9 April*

Your dear letter of the 7th/19th has reached me, dearest Annette. The contents touched me, enchanted me. The sentence you have expressed merit my blessing on you and God's. Persist in this noble course, in these elevated thoughts so worthy of you which assure a divine blessing and facilitate the way to solidarity. Just tell yourself that if I could love you any more I would now. Your letter was so sweet, so beneficial to my feelings that I wanted to share it with dear Nix, your old friend, who told me that he kissed your letter. I saw the Regiment of the Grenadiers leave today, exceedingly handsome.

### *Saturday 14 April*

The Declaration of War came out today, dear Annette. God bless and protect dear Nicholas. There is no motive of ambition in his plans but he cannot see his country suffer the disloyalty of these miserable Turks who no longer obey either law or good faith.

### *Tuesday 17 April*

Our dear little Alexander completes his tenth year today, God bless him. His birth made us very happy and fulfilled the wishes of the Empire. He is a very pleasant, charming child and everything he does, he does well. He looks marvellous on a horse and rides very well.

### *Thursday 19 April*

Michael arrived at 5:00 this morning. The morning was spent at a superb parade of the cavalry and the horse artillery which is here. William will tell you how fine they were. My regiment excelled. How pleased the Emperor is.

### *Tuesday 8 May*

My little half dozen arrived for dinner all pleased and in the best possible spirits. After dinner, after 7:00 in the evening William found the five youngest playing train at my place and me in the middle of them with my papers. I must say that it is a pleasure to have some time with these dear youngsters who are maturing so fast. Costa is the noisiest of them all. He has a loud voice and is always laughing, jumping, singing and talking in his own way. William was crazy over this little boy. Alexia has developed a passion for your husband. She told him that she loved him as much as her own Papa. Orange is her favourite colour and her little head has not forgottn the [predictions] which were made about her future. She is certainly a remarkable child, as beautiful as the day and so good. As well, she is very thoughtful, choosing her pastimes carefully and graceful in everything she does.

## Monday 14 May

I must thank you, my dear Annette, for your letter of May 2nd. I hasten to give your commission to dear William who, thank God, is well. To my regret, he is leaving us next Tuesday. He was perfect to me and really is a consoling angel. His presence was very dear to me and I admit that the thought of him leaving causes me a pang. Marie is also very happy to have William here. All these memories are locked in our hearts and if our tears often flow, at least we have good memories to think of. I see, dear Annette, that you are also very sad at the departure of the King and Queen and Marianne, but your dear William will soon be back with you. We spent all of our days in our family circle. Marie did not want — to see people before completing her sacred duty of visiting the fortress which I believe she is going to do Saturday.

## Monday 21 May

Dear William will tell you all the details which interest you but shall I tell you, my dear, about his leaving. My heart is broken. He was a consoling angel for me. When my sons left, he looked after me with a tenderness which I will never be able to repay. I beg you, my dear Annette, thank William for me again for all his goodness to me. His beautiful nature has again been demonstrated. . . . God give me the happiness of seeing him again, my dear, I have so little time left . . . that the happiness of being with one of my children is important to me.

## Tuesday 22 May

I am sending you, my dear, and ask you to accept with what pleasure you may, a malachite letter holder and a little malachite bell which I would like you to put on your writing table. It is coming by sea. I am also sending a little bracelet with a profile of Nicholas engraved as a cameo on an amethyst. It looks like him so I hope you will enjoy wearing it. I am sending you a work chest. I have one almost like it and William suggested that you would like to have one like mine. I hope these things will please you, my dear. William will tell you how much I liked your beautiful lace. I have another question, dear Annette, which it still pains me to raise. You remember that you copied your will in 1824 and since then things have changed. Our dear Angel, who was supposed to take it if I died, is no longer here. Tell me, dear Annette, should I send it back to you? Perhaps you would like to change it or confide it to other hands. Pardon me for referring to this which is so painful to me but I thought it was my duty.

## Pavlovsk
### *8 June*

The Emperor finds the country and the climate beautiful but he complains of the number of disgusting reptiles which the country is crawling with. That is all the news, my dear. The bulletin will be in the mail, a more direct way. We have enjoyed summer weather for the last four days but huge clouds are gathering already and we forecast a bad storm and heavy rain. But, thank God, the chances of good harvests look excellent. The countryside is superb and the vegetation magnificent and incredibly rich. Pavlovsk is very beautiful. Marie is enjoying it there and I tell myself that my dear Annette will enjoy it as much next year. The neighbourhood is enhanced by cultivation. My fields are very beautiful and I put land under cultivation as much as possible. I have some lovely flowers and the aubépine-French which has survived two winters in the open is in full flower. In the courtyard of the château, besides the laurels and orange trees, they have placed four beautiful palm trees. I am very proud of them. Surely no other fortress has palm trees except in Egypt. You see, my Anne, that I still have my passion for plants and flowers.

### *13 June*

The same evening, when I was returning home, my cousin, the King of Prussia, sent his aide-de-camp, Lendebourg[?], to announce the death of the dear Grand Duke of Weimar. Imagine my tears, my dear children, and my real sorrow. Our children had already retired so naturally I wanted to let them enjoy all the rest they could get. The next day was the birthday of their child, their son, and that of little Alexandrine. It would have been cruel to prevent Marie and Charles from enjoying the happiness associated with their son's birth. I therefore kept the whole weight of our sorrow to myself and only told my children the news after Mass. I suffered intolerably and my children saw an alteration in my expression which they could not explain. Finally, after Mass I told them but I had to announce it to Marie, Charles and August separately. Inexpressible sorrow and heartrending. It was a cruel day for me.

### Sunday 17 June

I congratulate you, my dear children, on the surrender of Brailov which the Emperor told me about yesterday evening. It came soon after an assault which did not allow for unforeseen events which human judgement could not have predicted. The man who exploded the first mine was unfortunately killed so there was no signal. Our troops, full of ardour, rushed forward believing that the wall was breached. Fortunately, Michael wisely stopped the assault but there were still many losses. The next day Michael exploded the other mine and the Turks asked to surrender. Dear Nicholas is very happy with the news, very pleased with our dear Michael and, according to the custom of the order and the court said that he would give him the Cross of St George. He would have been in despair at the failure of the assault and I must say that I weep for the victims but all the military people tell me the losses are insignificant in comparison to what they usually are and the importance of the place.

### Pavlovsk
### Wednesday 4 July

I must thank you, my dear child, for telling me of the visit of the King, Queen and Marianne. Did you think she was pleased and happy to be bespoke and was Prince Gustaf with them? I congratulate your little darling for her courage and think that you, dear William, holding her on your knee must have been trembling more than her. The dear girl must have a very sweet character to have borne the pain with such patience. Dear William, dear Annette, give her a fond kiss for me. Sasha's examinations have begun and I was notified and went there for eight hours. He answered very well and with consideration. I am going to return for the second part. It will take four days. All the children are well.

## *Tuesday 10 July*

I saw Duval, my dear, and the set of sapphire jewellry. He told me that he followed your wishes in sending it by a safe commercial route. I warned him that you might not take it, but that you wanted to see it and so did William before deciding whether to take it or send it back. The stones seem to be very beautiful.

## *Thursday 26 July*

My dear Annette, I am starting a letter to you today so that I will be able to give it to Prince Hohenlohe. I asked him to give the packet to Monsieur d' Anstadt telling him to send the letter to Ems if Helene is still there. If she has left, he is to write to William asking him where and how to address the packet. With these precautions I will allow myself to answer the warm letter you sent by courier, my dear child. I have a — to show that — in depth the story of Marianne's marriage with William. There is no more to [say] about it. One can only envisage Marianne's complete happiness and to ensure it, Prince Gustav [sic] must be able to count on the friendship of his beloved brother. Everything which happened on the day of the betrothal makes me very sorry for I know how sensitive dear William is and he was cruelly tried. I explained to him that his excellent mother, who loves him as much as Marianne, wanted him to be as thrilled as she is, acted that way because she expected him to feel as she does. Seeing that it was not so, she became upset about it and, because she is weak and unwell, her nerves get the better of her and so she gets overexcited which is not typical of her angelic disposition and her perfect love for William. It was not that she was angry in her heart but her nerves were irritated and she got carried away. It would be too bad if this episode left any trace on William's feeling for his adored mother. For goodness sake, my dear Anne, redouble your attention, your care, your affection for the good Queen. Believe me, she will appreciate it because it will prove that you want to show her that neither you nor William hold that moment of ill humour against her. The more her physical weakness increases, dear Anne, the more you should care for her. You would be returning attentions which she has lavished on you. The King's letter to William touched me and so did William's to the King. Both are so affectionate and good as they should be. In any case, I discussed all this in my letter to William. I asked him to show it to you so that I would not have to repeat myself. You behaved like an angel, my dear, on this occasion. With faith, tact, and smoothing things over as much as possible. In hastening to warn William, you were acting from the heart to spare him a disagreeable surprise. The King's behaviour is so friendly and affectionate that I am glad to know about it. Finally unity is of prime importance in this world and is the base of the security and peace of the state. I am sure, dear Annette, that you are good and affectionate to Marianne as well. Obviously she has given her heart to Prince Gustaf. We must hope for and desire her happiness. As for the gossip, it will fade as it always does when it is based on false propositions. I have sent your letter to the Emperor, dear Annette, as you wished.

## Pavlovsk
### *2 August*

After the Emperor had seen all the necessary preparations and examined the state of the fortress on the heights which we are living in, he embarked to go to our fleet which is before Worsi[?]. He inspected it, gave the necessary orders for the start of operations and then embarked on the frigate, *Flora*, which has 44 cannons and arrived in two days and 18 hours in front of the Empress' estate. Attracted to the window by the salutes which were given as they passed her dwelling, she noticed the imperial standard. Imagine her happiness when not long after she saw the barge bringing the Emperor and Michael. She received them at the pier in front of her house and there was great and mutual happiness. Thank God we can breathe now. At least we know Nik and Michael are together and resting a little after so much fatigue. He has taken a wise course. The blockades are set up and the Emperor should not stay there waiting for things to happen while doing nothing. So there is general joy in knowing that he is at Odessa. Dear children, here is the news which I received from our dear Nicki yesterday. He and the Empress are well. Our navy has won a new glory. Our galleons captured the Turkish galleons which were in the port of Varna in full view of the fortress in spite of the cannonade and spirited defence.

## Pavlovsk
### *17 August*

His campaign is glorious and lucky. The siege of Varna is continuing. At Schumla, the place is sealed off. There are small frays but nothing important will be undertaken before the guards arrive. The sultan persists, they say, in going for all or nothing. I think the arrival of French troops in the Crimea will force him to change his mood.

### *Friday 7 September*

We have beautiful sunny weather and I took advantage of it to go for a long walk. I had an interesting man here for dinner, my dear, the famous Captain Fresalin[?], who in 1821–22 and again in 1826 made the perilous trip to the shores of the Polar sea. His calm and reflective expression is that of the intrepid and noble character which he tested in bearing all the perils and evils of such a voyage. He is now tempted to begin a third.

### *Tuesday 2 October*

The dear Empress arrived here at Gatchina with Marie at 2:00 in the afternoon. Sasha and I went as far as the first station to meet her. The little man threw himself into his mother's arms, dissolving in tears. I am very happy to see Alexandrine and the little girl.

### *Saturday 6 October*

I hope that your stay at Tervuren, which William likes, as well as your stay in Brussels will improve his health as these are William's two favourite places. I believe, my dear child, that you will also enjoy it and will not show any regret at leaving Foudgère because that would trouble dear William. I am hoping for a courier so that I will have the opportunity of answering your dear letter. I can only repeat what I have often already told you: perseverance, the most even temper, gentleness and serenity are, my dear child, the most precious quality a woman can have.

### *Saturday 13 October*

I did not write to you yesterday, my dear, as I had an acute haemorrhoidal colic which tormented me. I feel much better today and I had a good night but Pfehl[?] wants me to take care of myself today. The description you have given of your house is delightful, especially as you portray William's elation and surprise at the gardens and terrace which he gave you. I read it with great pleasure.

### *15 October*

My dear Annette, our Nicki returned today and I am more than happy. Stupidly though, I have fallen down with a haemorrhoidal colic and fever which is already somewhat better but they will not let me write. Farewell my dear Annette, dear William, I send my kisses to your children and yours always heart and soul.

## Letter from Alexandra to Anna
### *Posted 24 October / 5 November 1828*

My poor Anne! Poor dear sister! Our dear good Maman exists no more! How can we bear the thought? Oh God! We thought by her good health that she would be with us for a long time yet to see our happiness! How could she succumb to such a short illness which at the beginning seemed so insignificant? Yes, it is in vain that we ask why! We are to be pitied. Poor Nicki feels it terribly and all of us who kissed her hand as she was dying, who received her last look. He is completely undone! And preaches acceptance to me when he does not have much himself! I send a kiss to dear William. He loved her, adored her as his own mother. Our ideas were in perfect harmony when we talked of her. We often used to say people do not know, they are not aware of everything she was for all of us! Ah! She will live in our hearts and collect the tenderness which we could not always express! I fear for your health, for William's! She hoped to see you next summer having decided that she would travel to Carlsbad and the idea of seeing you all was [pleasure] when she felt this melancholy that she had to cope with since this illness.

Signed
Alexandra

# Index

# Index